NEVER LOSE HEART

Never Lose Heart

Max Merritt Morrison

DOUBLEDAY & COMPANY, INC.

GARDEN CITY, NEW YORK

Library of Congress Catalog Card Number 64-19291
Copyright © 1964 by Max Merritt Morrison
All Rights Reserved
Printed in the United States of America

To my wife
LUCILE
with love and gratitude

PREFACE

The most pressing need of each one of us is to be able to face life without losing heart. Sometimes the need is more intensely felt than at other times. Such experiences have come to individuals in all ages of man's history.

However, it is unnecessary to remind us, living as we do in the second half of the turbulent twentieth century, that we are in the midst of a time when all the resources of our minds and souls are being severely tested. We need a steadying inner strength to enable us to stand up to life in an upset world.

The chapters which follow are written for those who are earnestly seeking such strength. With the desire to be helpful in a most practical way, I have tried to put what I have to say in a plain, straightforward, readable style.

If there is enkindled in only a few of the readers of this book such faith and courage that they can confidently affirm with the Apostle Paul, "I never lose heart!" then I shall feel I am happily rewarded.

Max Merritt Morrison

Pasadena, California
  February 1964

CONTENTS

NEVER LOSE HEART

CHAPTER ONE

KEEPING ENTHUSIASTIC ABOUT LIFE

The man who walked into my study was a stranger to me; I had never laid eyes on him before. He looked to be in his early forties, well groomed, acting a bit nervous, as though this were the first time he had ever been in a minister's study.

In a few introductory remarks he stated that he lived near Rosemead, that one day a month before, his business had brought him to Pasadena. Driving down Lake Avenue, he said, he noticed on our bulletin board my subject for the following Sunday. It appeared that the message might deal with the problem he was facing, so he resolved to attend our service of worship on Sunday.

He said he liked what he heard, and decided to come back the following week. He did so, and once more he said that he was helped. Though not a member of any church and not having attended one for a long time, and feeling he had no claim upon any minister's time, nevertheless he felt he had to come and talk with me.

After these few remarks by way of introduction, he paused for a moment, as if debating how he would begin. Then leaning forward he said:

"I'll come right to the point. My problem is that I am fed up with life, I'm sick of the whole cockeyed world. I'd just about decided that I wanted to chuck the whole business. There's no more use of living, but I don't know

(13)

what to do. In your messages I have heard, you have given me a few rays of hope, but I haven't quite made up my mind that I want to keep on living."

He appeared to be a man of physical vigor, so it wasn't ill health that had brought him to this state. Furthermore, there didn't seem to be anything wrong with him that suggested any mental derangement.

I asked him why it was that he, a youngish-looking person, just entering middle life, an able-bodied man, should reach such a conclusion.

"Oh, I don't know," he replied, "I've just been thinking things over, and there doesn't seem to be much profit in living. What is life, anyway? You get up in the morning, eat breakfast, go downtown, work all day, come home, eat dinner, watch TV, then go to bed. And next day the same thing all over again. What's the percentage in that? Do you know?"

He spent about an hour in my study and came back to see me two or three times afterward. I noted a marked improvement in his attitude toward life and toward himself, but I have never seen him since. Whether he got a fresh grip on himself and decided life is worth living, or resolved to go through with his original intention of ending it all, I suppose I shall never know.

Here is a man suffering from a malady that is familiar to all those who counsel with people. He had a bad case of boredom, from which, one eminent psychologist says about seven persons out of ten suffer most of the time.

Fight Boredom

A loss of enthusiasm for life is one of the curses of our time, and it is never far from any one of us.

A minister announced from the pulpit one Sunday morning that there would be a special meeting of the church's board at the close of the service. When the meeting was called to order, it was discovered that a total stranger was present.

The minister explained that there must be some mistake as this was a meeting of the church's board. The man apologized by saying that when the minister announced a meeting of the "bored" he thought it was meant for him, because no one in the congregation was more bored than he.

There are those who are bored with their jobs, bored with their lot, bored with their husband or wife, bored with their town, or just bored in general. Nothing more unfortunate can happen to any person than to lose his enthusiasm for life, and sink into boredom.

One of the greatest mysteries I encounter in this world is a person who is bored. How any human being can live in this fascinating world of ours and be bored is too mysterious for me to attempt to understand. My most disturbing thought is that there are not enough years left in my life to see all the things I want to see, read all the books I want to read, meet all the people I want to meet.

Some become afflicted with the malady of boredom early in life, while others maintain their enthusiasm for life far into old age and to the end of life.

Some time ago there appeared in the newspapers the story of a young girl of twenty-one who committed suicide and left this note behind: *"I am 21. I have seen everything worth seeing. I know everything worth knowing. I don't like life—it's cheap, dirty, disappointing. I've had all I want."*

About the same time the press carried the story of a banquet held in Ontario, Canada, honoring Sir William Mulock on his ninety-fifth birthday. Sir William Mulock had served in the Canadian Parliament, had been Chief

Justice of the Supreme Court of Ontario, and Vice-Chancellor of the University of Toronto.

After various tributes had been paid this eminent statesman, jurist, and educator, the ninety-five-year-old Sir William, smiling and serene, got up to acknowledge the thunderous ovation. His voice was firm and clear as he spoke, the voice of a man who loved life, who loved his work and his fellow man. Among other things this is what he said:

"I am still at work, with my hand to the plow, and my face to the future. The shadows of evening lengthen about me, but morning is in my heart. The testimony I bear is this: That the Castle of Enchantment is not yet behind me. It is before me still, and daily I catch glimpses of its battlements and towers. The best of life is always further on. Its real lure is hidden from our eyes, somewhere behind the hills of time."

The speech was widely printed and discussed in Canadian and American newspapers and magazines at the time. One newspaper writer declared: "Every man over forty should carry a copy of Sir William's speech in his pocket." Said another: "His zest for life, his unfailing courage and good cheer, put many a younger man to shame."

Sir William Mulock died five years later at the age of one hundred. He enjoyed a rich and rewarding life to the end.

What was the difference between the twenty-one-year-old girl and the stranger who came to my study on the one hand and the great Canadian, Sir William Mulock, on the other hand? The difference is that of losing or keeping one's enthusiasm for life.

Feel Joy Inside

Once I was leading a service of worship for a group of young people and was reading the 114th Psalm. When I came to the fourth verse of that psalm which reads: "The mountains skipped like rams, the hills like lambs," I paused and asked: "Did any of you ever see the hills skip like lambs?"

They looked at me as though they thought I had suddenly "slid off my rocker." One boy spoke up and said: "I never have. I've never been that drunk."

When I told them that I had seen the mountains skip like lambs—and I was not drunk at the time—they were sure that I had "lost my marbles," as one of them expressed it.

But then I explained that I had "seen" such a phenomenon in the sense in which the psalm writer was referring. It was the Oriental's familiar way of symbolizing the way he felt on the inside. He felt a great joy inside, and all nature seemed to respond to his feeling.

It was the way Maltbie Babcock must have felt when he wrote:

> This is my Father's world,
> And to my listening ears,
> All nature sings, and round me rings
> The music of the spheres.
>
> This is my Father's world:
> He shines in all that's fair,
> In the rustling grass I hear Him pass,
> He speaks to me everywhere.[1]

Jesus of Nazareth has too often been pictured in art, described in literature and proclaimed from the pulpit as "a man of sorrows and acquainted with grief." I do not wish to enter into a theological argument at this point, but I am convinced that the writer of the 53rd chapter of

[1] From *Thoughts for Everyday Living* by Maltbie D. Babcock (New York: Charles Scribner's Sons, 1901).

Isaiah was not referring to Jesus when he wrote those words: "A man of sorrows and acquainted with grief."

In a sense He was a man of sorrows, but it was not His own sorrows. He sorrowed over men's lack of understanding of life—that it was to be lived and enjoyed and used to the glory of God.

He was acquainted with grief, but it was not His own grief. He grieved over the pains and heartaches which came upon people because of their mistaken actions, He grieved over man's inhumanity to his fellow man.

But above everything else, Jesus was a man of great joy, who had a great zest for living and tried to transmit that enthusiasm for life to others. Wherever the Master went, the most familiar words on His lips were: "Be not afraid," and "Be of good cheer."

A Boston newspaper once printed this item: "The day was dark and gloomy but Phillips Brooks walked down through Newspaper Row and all was bright."

That could have been said with greater truth of Jesus. Wherever He went life became different, more radiant, more worthwhile to those He met and served. That is the reason we call His message "the Gospel," which is an abbreviation of the words "the Good News."

One of the things that seemed to concern Jesus deeply was the lack of zestful living so prevalent all about Him. People were burdened down by worry, care, hurry, and strain, even as we are today.

He taught three great truths about enthusiastic, radiant, happy living.

Change Your Thoughts

First of all, He taught that the sources of enthusiastic living are within us, and not outside of us. "The kingdom of heaven is within you," said Jesus. It is a state of mind; it is uncovered and sustained by your thoughts.

It is something we experience within our own consciousness. It is produced not by objects, but by ideas, thoughts, and attitudes which can be developed by the individual's own choices.

A class in physiology had been studying the working of the various organs of the body—the heart, the liver, the lungs, and the stomach. One day a little girl brought the teacher a note from her mother in which she wrote: *"Dear teacher: I don't want my Mary to learn anything more about her insides."*

What goes on inside Mary's body is important, but later on in some class, not in physiology but in psychology or religion, it is hoped that she will learn the importance of what goes on inside her mind. It is hoped she will discover that our reactions to the circumstances of life are determined by the thoughts we live with, the faiths we live by, the images we cherish in our minds, the things we love.

All these determine the way in which we live, the way in which we meet the circumstances of life. One of the wisest reflections of that great philosopher-emperor, Marcus Aurelius, was this: "Your life is what your thoughts make it."

Another wise man, Emerson, said it another way: "Our life is what we think about all day long." But an ancient Hebrew writer, who lived long before Marcus Aurelius or Emerson, put the same thought this way: "As a man thinketh in his heart, so is he."

One morning the five-year-old son of a doctor overheard his father tell his mother: "I have been called out on a maternity case and I do not know when I shall be home."

A few minutes later the doorbell rang and the little lad answered. "Is the doctor in?" inquired the caller.

"No sir," the little lad replied.

"Have you any idea when he will be back?" the man asked.

"I don't know, sir," the boy answered. "He went out on an eternity case."

Each of us is working on an "eternity case"—the future destiny not only of ourselves but the world in which we live—and the most important tool we use in the operation is thought. What we think, what we have been thinking for a long time, and what we are going to think tomorrow will determine what we are and the kind of world we live in.

What the ancient Hebrew sage, Marcus Aurelius, and Emerson are trying to tell us is that we can change our lives and our world by changing our thoughts. If we are to regain our lost zest for life the adventure must begin within us. The choice is ours to make.

Abraham Lincoln said that "most people are about as happy as they make up their minds to be." Jesus taught that men and women have as much zest for living as they make up their minds—that is, their thoughts—to have.

Think of Others

In the second place, Jesus taught that one maintains an enthusiastic interest in life by losing one's life in a concern for others.

If you could look into the lives of all the frustrated, unhappy people you have known, you will find that the root cause of it all is self-absorption. Taking a genuine interest in other people, striving to make them happy, helping them to find meaning in life, is one of the best ways of finding it ourselves.

Of all the people I have known, certainly Mary Matthews is remembered as one who lived for others. She was born and reared in a wealthy, cultured New England home. As a young woman she fell in love with a home missionary, who had just accepted a teaching position on the faculty of a little church college in the southwestern part of our country, when it was new and undeveloped.

Against the protests of her parents and the advice of her friends, she married the young teacher and went to share his life and make a home in that section of the country, which was at the time far out on the frontiers of our country.

Before she arrived on the campus of the little college, the young men and women from the pioneer homes had been spending four years there, many of them less, then returning to their homes and settling down to the same way of life their forebears had known.

But Mary Matthews brought to them visions of the great world beyond limited horizons and opened their minds to their own unlimited possibilities. Seeing a young woman with musical ability, she encouraged her to strive for perfection. Seeing a young man with gifts of speech, she held before him a mental picture of great audiences listening to his words, or juries being moved by his eloquence. Seeing a boy with a talent for scientific research, she inspired him with thoughts of high achievement.

She fired each of them with the glory of human service, and helped them see life's heights and far horizons. So the students began to graduate from that little college and go out to take places of leadership throughout the world —businessmen, ministers, teachers, scientists, statesmen, judges, artists, and musicians.

Mary Matthews lived on the campus with her husband until his death, then for more than twenty-five years longer near the campus. But on the campus or off the campus, her home was always open to the students, who came to visit her singly and in groups to bask in the warmth and radiance of her personality. In the later years of her life she was the friend and counselor of the grandchildren of some of the students who were in college when she arrived on the campus as a young bride more than three quarters of a century before. She died at the age of ninety-three, still interested in life, the world about her, and especially in young people and their needs.

Mary Matthews could have wasted her life away with self-pity over her lot in life. She could have pulled her skirts about her and withdrawn into herself as a protest against the lack of cultural advantages to be found on the frontier. But instead, she refused to let her life grow in upon herself—she extended it outward into the lives of others. In forgetting herself, she found herself—a larger, more zestful, happier self.

Commit Yourself to God's Will

A third thing that Jesus taught is that lasting zest for life can only come as we commit ourselves to the will of God. "In His will is our peace," said Dante.

What an exhaustless source of supply Jesus drew upon for His love of life! It was nothing less than an "all out" trust in God. From this source of supply there flowed His boundless hope for the future, His consciousness that He had found and was doing God's will for His life, His sense of God's approval upon His life, and His knowledge that He was doing a great and abiding service for mankind.

Jesus lived in an upset world, but He taught us the ultimate secret of finding life good, and of living zestfully. It is to yield yourself to God at the deepest level of your life.

It will keep you everlastingly alive, vibrant, eager, and enthusiastic!

CHAPTER TWO

OVERCOMING THE FEELING OF FUTILITY

When a circus comes to town, I am drawn to the show grounds as by a magnet! Since my boyhood days, everything under the "big top" has had an endless fascination for me. The prancing horses, the man on the flying trapeze, the lion tamer, the clowns, the music of the band, and all the rest creates in me a breathless excitement like no other form of entertainment I know.

At the last circus I attended the feature act was a troupe of jugglers handling six Indian clubs. One juggler took the clubs from a trunk and began to toss them into the air and catch them. After a few seconds he seemed to tire of tossing them about, and just turned around and walked away, leaving the clubs suspended in the air.

Before the clubs could hit the ground, another juggler stepped up and took his partner's place, and began catching and tossing the same clubs. After a while, he nonchalantly waved his hand and walked off, leaving the clubs in the air, and at this point No. 1 again became active, and without dropping a single club, took up where No. 2 had left off.

They went through this routine for some time, and finally, one of them caught the clubs and put them back into the trunk. And that's all they ever did with them—just took turns tossing the clubs about. They used them for no other purpose.

(23)

Now that's all right when it comes to Indian clubs, but life should not be treated like that. Some people take life as casually as the juggler takes his Indian clubs. They pick up life, toss it about for a period of years without any particular purpose, then lay it aside at death. Some are bored with life, some are afraid of it, while others just live to no purpose.

One day in a city park, while strolling down a winding walk fringed with flowers, I came upon a beautiful water fountain. In the center of the fountain was a marble statue of a young nymph and behind the statue a high rock. From the top of the rock there flowed a thin stream of water which arched and fell into the open outstretched hand of the young woman in marble. There she stood day after day with the water slipping aimlessly through her fingers, none of it ever lifted to her lips, or offered to a thirsty passerby.

Of course, she was lifeless and could not help herself, but the marble nymph set disturbing thoughts in my mind. She reminded me of so many men and women and young people I know—people who are not made of marble, but of flesh and blood—who let life slip through their fingers like water, and who either do not care, or seem to be powerless to do anything about it.

Have a Reason for Living

This problem is well stated in the words of a young man who once came to the minister's study. His moral life was in a shambles, he had lost his ambition, and had come to the conclusion that existence was not worth the effort. He was so in doubt about the purpose of everything that he felt it was useless to do anything at all. "The trouble with me," he confessed in all honesty to the minister, "is I have no reason for living. An aimless existence is fit for an animal, but a man needs a reason, and I have none."

The case of this young man is no isolated incident. How often one who counsels with individuals meets people like that, adults and young people, for whom everything has grown futile. They have come to believe that they are of no consequence, and are quite convinced that their lives count for nothing. They arise in the morning with a feeling of frustration, and go to bed at night assured that they have accomplished nothing of significance. For them life is a dead-end street.

The sense of futility that crowds so many lives to the wall today is in reality born of aimless living. We have too much random living because we refuse to commit ourselves to anything beyond ourselves. Frustration, inner strain and wishful thinking are the results.

I have counseled with hundreds of adults and young people across the years, and I believe that I have listened to all the problems that disturb human beings. In counseling with people who are a problem to themselves, I have discovered that no matter how their difficulty may have started, it became most acute at that point where they began to doubt that life has any meaning. None of them ever finds a satisfactory answer to the problem until he or she discovers a reason for living.

The Little Acts of Kindness

Any one tormented by a feeling of futility should read the little book by David Dunn, with the intriguing title: *Try Giving Yourself Away.*[1]

David Dunn is a successful, hard-working businessman. His business interests keep him traveling to all parts of this great country.

[1] Scarsdale, N. Y.: The Upgraff Press, Ltd.

But one day he began to be disturbed with the thought that life was not working out well for him, and that there was a great deal of uncertainty and unhappiness in the modern world. He had begun to feel that life had lost its luster and its meaning. Somehow in the shuffle of things he had lost his reason for living.

One night he was on the *Twentieth Century Limited* going from Chicago to New York, and had just retired to his compartment bed. Before dropping off to sleep he began to think about being a passenger on that very famous train of the New York Central—the *Twentieth Century Limited.*

He remembered that there was another *Limited* that left New York, too, just as this one was leaving Chicago. Mr. Dunn said to himself: "I wonder where these *Century* trains pass in the night?" The idea fascinated him: "Where the *Centuries* pass."

So the morning after his arrival in New York, he wrote a letter to the New York Central, in which he said: "I have this little idea, it is yours, there is nothing involved at all, it is yours gladly: Where do the *Centuries* pass each other?"

In a few days he received a letter from an official of the railroad, who informed him that those two great trains passed each other eight miles west of Buffalo.

So the New York Central capitalized on the idea. Now, Mr. Dunn says, wherever he travels, not only in this country, but in Europe, in the express offices he sees that beautiful picture entitled, "Where the Centuries Pass."

It is the picture of a great powerful locomotive with huge blinding headlights, while the rear of the other *Century* is seen with the rear platform brilliantly lighted— one going to Chicago, the other to New York—passing in the night.

That incident started David Dunn's hobby of "giving

himself away." His book is a series of incidents about what happened to him and his outlook on life when he found that hobby.

One incident occurred as follows: Mr. Dunn was going by an attractive department store window one day. He looked at the artistry and beauty of it, and said: "I must go in and compliment the manager of that store." So he went in and asked for the manager. It took time, and he was giving it away.

When the manager came, Mr. Dunn said to him: "I would like to compliment the decorator of your windows. I am not interested in buying a thing, but I just wanted to take time to tell you that it is a beautiful display." The manager looked at him in amazement and thanked him.

Mr. Dunn went on his way, but sometime later he received a letter from a young man who wrote: "Because of your kindness in stopping to tell our manager that you liked my window display, I have been advanced in position and receive $20.00 a week increase in salary."

Mighty influences possibly developed for the young decorator out of a simple act of kindness performed by one man who took time to give away his time.

No wonder David Dunn found meaning in life. The Apostle Paul could not have spoken more truly, if he had been talking about this very thing, when he wrote: "He that soweth sparingly shall reap sparingly, and he that soweth bountifully shall reap bountifully."

It is one of the strange paradoxes of human experience that he who gives himself away most completely has more of himself to give, and, as a by-product, discovers a real reason for living.

Albert Schweitzer's Reward

There is one class of people you never hear raising the question as to whether life is worth living. They are the people who are sacrificially giving not only their time but their very lives in human service. They are too busy serving the needs of others and trying to make this a better world in which to live to stop and ask the question: "Is life worth living?"

Some years ago Dr. Albert Schweitzer, accompanied by his wife, arrived in this country to deliver an important lecture on the German poet, Goethe, at Aspen, Colorado. They were met by a group of newspaper reporters when their ship docked in New York. Dr. Schweitzer was asked whether he thought it worth his time and effort for a man of his genius to give up a life among his intellectual peers in Europe and bury himself among the savages of Africa "on the edge of the primeval forest."

Dr. Schweitzer's answer was, "I have had the pleasure of doing good. That is privilege enough for any man."

Ask the Right Question

Too many people fail to find a reason for living because they approach life asking the wrong question, "What do I want?" rather than "What is wanted of me?"

Waterloo Place in London is characterized by its banks and insurance offices. But its most striking feature is a group of monuments and statues commemorating the Crimean War of 1854-55. In the center is the Guards' Monument, on the right a statue of Lord Herbert of Lea, who was the secretary of war during the campaign, and on the left a statue of Florence Nightingale, "The Lady with the Lamp," as she was known.

If one is at all sensitive to the long history of mankind's struggle to make life on this planet more humane, it is a moving experience to look upon that statue of Florence Nightingale and to recall the major role she played and, through her influence, still plays in the relief of human suffering.

As I stood one day looking at her statue there in Waterloo Place, I found myself reflecting upon that great woman's life. She was born and reared in a home where she had everything she needed for life, except the most important thing, which money cannot buy: a purpose for living. And not until she looked at the desperate state of the nursing profession in her day and asked the question "What is wanted of me?" did she discover who Florence Nightingale really could become. And in answering that question she found a purpose for her life.

Find Opportunities for a Better World

"But," you say, "I am not made of the same stuff as Albert Schweitzer or Florence Nightingale. I don't have their physical energy, their intellectual ability or their spiritual insight. Because of the circumstances of my life I can't go to faraway places like Africa or the Crimea and serve on such a grand scale."

But one does not have to leave his own community to find opportunities to help a better world come into being. There are many places near at hand calling for you. There are social agencies in your town which are in need of volunteer workers. There is the P.T.A. What greater investment in the present and the future could you make than through teaching a class of children or young people in your church. There are lonely people on every street, shut-ins, cripples who need someone to give them a little encouragement or a helping hand. There are groups trying to right the wrongs in every community that need you.

Many people fail to find a reason for living because they approach life asking the wrong question: "What do I want?" That question has never discovered anyone's destiny. It is in finding the answer to the question "What is wanted of me?" that one finds a real meaning for one's life.

It is the surrender of oneself to something beyond self and greater than self which gives life its glory and makes it worth living. The Great Teacher of Galilee said: "He that loses his life shall find it." Yes, he shall find it a greater, happier, and more significant life!

CHAPTER THREE

MAKING THE BEST OF A BAD SITUATION

The writer of the 84th Psalm says: "Happy are they who, strengthened by Thee, set out on pilgrimage! When they pass through the Valley of Baca they make it a place of springs."

If there was such a Valley of Baca in Palestine, it must have been rather small and obscure, because it does not appear on maps of that country. The word "baca" means "weeping" and may refer to a valley filled with balsam trees, which, because such trees exude beads of gum, resembling tears, was called "Valley of Weeping."

In any case, in the 84th Psalm the phrase figuratively but plainly points to the typical experience of sorrow turned into joy, of despair into hope, of defeat into victory.

Make Your Own Places of Springs

Each of us finds himself at times in the Valley of Baca. The way we make the journey through that valley in our earthly pilgrimage depends upon the attitude of mind we bring to it. The same experience of limitation, despair, or defeat comes to different people, but some, in passing through their Valley of Baca have made it a place of springs.

We engage in much talk about the effect of our environment upon our conduct. Environment does play a great part in our moral conditioning. I remind you that I am aware of that fact. And I would not have the truth I am setting forth here seem to contradict that fact.

But there is another fact we need to remember as well: we also do things to our environment. And what our environment does to us or we do to it, depends largely upon the attitude of mind we bring with us as we face our environment.

There are several areas of experience where this truth is seen operating. I know a young man who sat in a class where the professor's lectures were so dry and uninteresting that every time he came out of the classroom this young man said that he felt like he had been taking a bath in the hot sands of the Sahara Desert. But he so wanted to become a thorough student in the subject that he went into the library each day and read all the books and magazines he could find on the subject. Then in spite of the fact that he spent more time in class catching up on his sleep than he did in listening to the lecture, he passed the course with honors.

Now he was not the first or the last student who sat under a dull teacher. Many other students under similar circumstances have lost interest in the course and blamed it all on the teacher. But this young man passing through the Valley of Baca made it a place of springs.

Every day we are witnesses of what one can do to his environment in the world of business. Here are two men I know in the banking business. One tells me that he hates the work. He despises, what he calls, the everlasting feeling that he is being checked up on. He resents having to be courteous to an irritating public.

He wishes that he had been wise enough as a youth to have chosen a different business. And even now, he says, at this late date he would chuck the banking business, if he could find another business that has as many holidays.

Making the Best of a Bad Situation

But there is this other banker friend of mine, who has to put up with the same disagreeable aspects, and has to deal with the same irritating public. However, he says that if he had his life to live over again, he would still choose the banking business. He gets a thrill out of being a part of the ongoing commercial enterprises of our great country and especially of his community.

There again we see the difference in the attitude of mind with which a situation can be faced.

An interesting book by Henno Martin is entitled *The Sheltering Desert*. In a brief review of the book, the critic said: "For two and a half years, the author lived in the Nambib Desert of Africa. Here, in one of the most barren places in the world, he relived the life of stone-age men, tracking down water holes and game, improvising housing like a modern Robinson Crusoe."

Then comes this closing sentence: "His is the tale of a man who took a desolate land and made it home." In other words, he took a geographical Valley of Baca and made it a place of springs.

How can you take your desert experience in life and make it your spiritual friend rather than let it become your spiritual enemy?

It's Your Reaction That Counts

For one thing, you can look around within your Valley of Baca itself for the resources with which to triumph over its desolation. Make it contribute the help you need to overcome itself.

Some never find springs in the desert of despair, sorrow or disaster, because they never look for them. They are quite sure they are not there so they keep their eyes on the distant horizon looking for some caravan to bring them refreshment from afar.

Or with parched tongue, they chase, across the burning sands, dancing mirages which bring them nothing but bitterness and despair. Their time is consumed with wishful thoughts that perhaps conditions might be better elsewhere.

There was a railroad junction in New England in the mid-nineteenth century called Essex Junction. If one was scheduled to change trains there, it usually meant a layover of the better part of a day. That little railroad junction came in for some very bitter comments from travelers who had occasion to journey that way.

I am certain that the nineteenth-century poet Edward John Phelps must have sensed the impatience of many weary travelers, who were forced to spend a day waiting for a train at Essex Junction, when he expressed the fervent hope that whoever invented that dreary place would have their souls consigned to perdition when they died.

But there was one traveler who did not agree with the critics of Essex Junction. Under the date of August 16, 1868, Ralph Waldo Emerson penned these words in his journal: *"On Wednesday I spent the day at Essex Junction, and traversed the banks and much of the bed of the Winooski River, much admiring the falls, and the noble mountain peaks of Mansfield, and the view of the Adirondacks across the lake."*

Both Emerson and Phelps faced the same experience —long hours of waiting in the same undesirable place. What caused the difference in their reactions? Was it not the difference in the mental attitude each brought to the experience? One found resources within that undesirable place which enabled him to triumph over its seeming desolation, and the other did not. Passing through that dreary Valley of Baca, called Essex Junction, Emerson made it a place of springs.

Making the Best of a Bad Situation

And thus it has ever been. Twelve spies were sent into the land of Canaan to bring back a report to Moses on the prospects of the Israelites taking the land. Ten saw nothing but giants, while two saw a land flowing with milk and honey.

Two boys were sent to hunt wild grapes. One was happy because they found the grapes, the other was unhappy because they had seeds in them.

Two little girls were examining a bush. One observed that it had thorns on it, and so called it a thorn bush. The other saw roses on the bush and so called it a rose bush.

Two men went to a large city. One visited the taverns, the brothels, and the gambling houses, and thought the city wicked. The other visited the churches, the homes, the symphony concerts, and the art galleries, and thought the city good.

"Two men look through their prison bars, one sees the mud, the other sees the stars."

To one man Essex Junction is a place of despair; to another it offers an opportunity to enjoy a delightful experience with nature.

A young Army officer said: "Weather, in time of war, is always favorable, if you know how to use it." That is just the point, "if you know how to use it." The fact is that everything that comes to you in life is favorable—if you know how to use it.

Life is determined perhaps more by reactions than by actions. Life comes to you without acting, it forces situations upon you without your asking. It is then that the reaction counts.

You can react in self-pity and in frustration. Or you can react with confidence and courage and can make the evil thing make you better. Its origin may be evil, but by the time it gets through you its destination may be good—you

have turned evil into good, you have made your Valley of
Baca a place of springs.

Salvage Life's Leftovers

In the second place, if you are going to make your Valley
of Baca into a place of refreshment, you need to learn how
to salvage the waste materials of life. Someone has said
that one of the secrets of a good cook is knowing how to
take the leftovers from one meal and prepare another one
out of them.

They have learned how to do this in the industrial
world. Whole industries have been built up by salvaging
of waste materials which formerly were thrown into the
discard. Fortunes have been made out of leftovers.

Just so in this business of living, it is a great art, worth
cultivating, to know how to salvage the leftovers after
disaster, sorrow, and disappointment have done their
worst.

I am thinking now of a young woman who did just that.
She was born with a harelip and a cleft palate. She was so
frail in childhood that she was not expected to live. A
weakness had threatened to make her half blind, and although her eyesight had been saved it had been necessary to practice lifelong caution in the use of her eyes.

In addition to all this, a hearing difficulty developed
and became permanent. Because of her general frailty,
she had in childhood been kept from association with other
children in play, and not permitted to go to school until
several years after the normal time.

But even at the early age of ten she began to take herself in hand sturdily. She begged to go to school as other
children were doing. Her parents were entirely willing to
educate and care for her at home, but she preferred, in

spite of her conspicuous handicaps, to mingle with other children and take from them whatever she must take.

Because of her speech difficulty, she could but rarely be given a chance to recite at school, and the learning of foreign languages was fraught with exceptional difficulty. But she persisted. She insisted on going to college, in spite of the opposition of her family.

After graduation she planned for a professional course, but because of her handicaps the school refused to enroll her. Again her sturdy persistence won the day. By securing the endorsement of her former teachers, she was finally given a chance.

When the professional course came to an end, there was difficulty once again. Her faculty advisers did nothing to help her secure a position. She secured one by her own refusal to accept defeat.

The disfiguring deformity has been repaired and is not too apparent, but she has to wear an artificial palate in her throat continually, and do all her talking with the aid of that. Today, she is a successful professional woman, highly respected in her community, and a Christian leader in her city.

In thinking of her, one likes to remember a word of Marcus Aurelius: "It is a shameful thing for the soul to faint while the body still perseveres."

Here was a soul that would not faint. She salvaged the little that life gave her and made something great out of it. She demonstrated that the abundance of life can be dragged out of the apparent defeat of life.

Such has always been the strategy of the brave. When life's road gets rough, and there are sharp stones in their path, they go on with bleeding feet through their Valley of Baca, making it a place of springs. They push on doing hard things, noble things, in spite of their bleeding feet and the ache in their hearts.

Like George Eliot, bitterly disappointed in love, they go on writing books, wiser for their anguish. Like John Milton, struck blind, they go on pouring out their souls in poetry.

Like Sir Harry Lauder, after his son was killed on the Western Front in World War I, or Joe E. Brown, after his son was killed in World War II, they march on singing for the sake of others who need their laughter and their songs.

Dare to Trust God

But up to this point we have been emphasizing the second part of this word from the 84th Psalm. It is when one looks at the first part of the statement that he comes to the heart of the matter: "Happy are they," says the Psalmist, "who, strengthened by Thee set out on pilgrimage. When they pass through the Valley of Baca they make it a place of springs."

"Strengthened by Thee." It is faith in God, in His strength, His active power and love, that gives us the final triumph over life's circumstances.

We Christians ought to be ashamed of ourselves for going to pieces the way we do. Let others lose their heads, become hysterical and pessimistic if they will, but Christians ought to keep their mental and spiritual balance. It is a sad commentary on our lack of faith that we don't.

Perhaps our trouble is that, in spite of our professed faith, we think we can manage all right by ourselves, if we try hard enough, but that isn't the case. Too often we try hard, and go on the rocks for all our trying.

Like a frightened child trying to learn to swim, we struggle until we sink from sheer exhaustion. All the while, we ought to know that, even though much depends upon ourselves, the water can be trusted to do much more

—sustain us by a glorious buoyancy, whose generous strength knows no limitations.

God's everlasting arms are something more than a figment of a poet's imagination—they are as real as the stars are real. To be sure we do not find them until we dare to lean upon their strength.

But then, did ever a beginner believe the water to be his friend? What fearful splasher in the shallow end of the pool ever believed the water would not let him sink? He strikes off into the deep water only when he dares to trust the water to hold him up.

You and I have our lives held together, and are kept afloat, only when we go beyond our own resources, our own courage, and dare to trust God. We have to learn to let go, and let God.

Once upon a time there was a young man who had such a faith. He lived without fear, even though circumstances forced Him into a desolating Valley of Baca experience, and His enemies nailed Him to a cross.

But not one word of self-pity passed His lips. He was conscious in His valley of pain of a great Presence surrounding and pervading His life.

Listen to that young man as He talks to this Presence and calls Him Father: "Father, if it be Thy will, let this cup pass from me—nevertheless, not my will but Thine be done" . . . "Father, forgive them, they know not what they do" . . . "Father, into Thy hands I commit my spirit."

Jesus so used His Valley of Baca, His cross, that He has been the moving spirit in the life of civilized man across the centuries. He turned disaster into triumph through His faith in God.

And how about you? I know not the circumstances of life you may be facing, what Valley of Baca you are passing through. But this I do know: However dark life may look to you, however hopeless the future seems, victory can come to you through an active faith in God.

Strengthened by His might in your inner life, you can face your Valley of Baca in such a courageous manner that it will cease being your spiritual enemy, and become your spiritual friend.

CHAPTER FOUR

HAVING THE COURAGE TO ENDURE

He was just a frail little fellow, about five feet, three inches tall, and weighing less than 115 pounds. Because of his size, the boys nicknamed him "Peewee."

He graduated from high school in 1933, one of the blackest years of the great depression. He enrolled in the state university, where he planned to study for a degree in engineering.

Peewee's mother had been divorced when he was two years of age, leaving him and a brother four years older for her to support. She worked at odd jobs, many of them, and at the time Peewee was attending high school she was a clerk in a large department store.

Since he had been old enough to work, Peewee had engaged in odd jobs during the summer, and on Saturdays during the winter. When he left for the university his mother gave him $35, the only money he ever received from her during his college career.

Because he was willing to make any kind of sacrifices for an education, he did jobs of every kind on the university campus. He washed dishes for twenty-five cents an hour, mowed lawns, and took care of babies for the professors' wives.

He could not afford to join a fraternity. He saw boys with whom he had been intimate in high school join fraternities, enlarge their interests, make new friends, and forget him. He confessed to me that one of the hardest things he had to bear was the growing indifference of his former friends.

One of these boys got into serious financial trouble and because he feared the consequences, kept it a secret from the folks at home. He came to Peewee, and the little fellow shared his hard-earned pittance with him.

After a few months, many boys and girls had to give up their college careers and return home because of the decreasing income of their fathers, who were facing the onslaught of the depression. But Peewee stayed on, working at the odd jobs which many of his former friends were too proud to do.

When the university closed for the summer, he returned home to face another test of courage and endurance. He began to tramp the streets and invade places of business in search of work. He was met by one disappointment after another.

Instead of taking on new workers, men were being laid off. The streets were crowded with the unemployed.

Because of the intense heat of the summer, the worry, and the fact that he was eating only one meal per day, he lost weight. He refused to let his mother help him.

He finally gave up the search for a job and tried to enlist in the Navy. His physical examination proved him unfit. He was found to be not only underweight, but one shoulder was higher than the other, his feet were flat, and his teeth bad. Outside of these deficiencies, he laughingly reported to me later, he was a perfect specimen.

He was so weak from undernourishment and worry over his failures that he fainted in the arms of the examining physician. Of course he was not accepted for the Navy.

There was nothing for him to do but go back to walking the streets again in search of work. At last he got a break:

a department store manager hired him to do the work of an assistant janitor.

He worked twelve hours a day for twenty-five cents an hour, and was so tired at the end of the day that he could not take off his clothes at times, but flopped on the bed and went to sleep dressed in his work clothes. Nonetheless he saved enough money to start college the next fall, so back to the doing of odd jobs on the campus once more.

During the Christmas holidays he again worked at the department store. He got up at five o'clock in the morning and cooked breakfast for himself and his older brother, and started to work at six o'clock.

He said that one of his greatest sorrows was his older brother's attitude toward life. He was always sitting around waiting for something easy to come his way.

Just before leaving for the university at the close of the Christmas holidays, a businessman—very much interested in Peewee—told him that he would see him through the university financially if he would change from his engineering course to a commercial course. Peewee declined his generous offer of assistance, because he had set his ambition to become an engineer.

During each of the four years of his university course, the experiences of Peewee were similar to those I have related of his first year. After he graduated, he came back to his home city and secured a position in an engineering firm.

I had the privilege of performing the wedding ceremony when Peewee took a lovely girl to be his wife. Across the years, I have lost track of Peewee, but if it is true that "the boy is father of the man," I have no doubt that he is a success at whatever he may be doing.

Through all his hard experiences Peewee never lost his faith in God, his radiant good cheer, his wholesome sense of humor, and his undying courage.

It was that last, his courage, that gives us the key to his life. He had the courage to stand up and take it. And when life knocked him down, he came up fighting again.

The Quiet Fortitude to Endure

Such courage as that displayed by my young friend, is not that aggressive daring of a soldier going into battle, or a federal officer walking into the hideout of a gangster. But it is the quiet fortitude to endure against hardships. It is a bravery which enables one to fight year after year against poverty, hunger, disappointments, and hardships, and not give up.

Centuries ago a New Testament writer said, in describing the heritage of his people: "Some became mighty in war, others suffered chains and imprisonment."

There are the two contrasting situations life creates, and there are the two contrasting types of courage appropriate to them. The first is the courage to conquer: "Some became mighty in war." The second is the courage to endure: "Others suffered chains and imprisonment."

The courage of Peewee and all his kind is the courage to endure. This is the kind of courage life calls for most often. Very few pass through life without being called upon some time to exhibit the courage of endurance.

Douglas Malloch might have dedicated his poem to "Peewee" and all his kind:

> Courage is not just
> To bare one's bosom to a sabre thrust
> In sudden daring—
> Courage is to grieve
> O'er many secret wounds, and make believe
> You are not caring.

Having the Courage to Endure

Courage does not lie
In dying for a cause. To die
Is only giving—
Courage is to feel
The daily daggers of persistent steel
And keep on living.[1]

I am sure that I am not wrong when I say that this kind of courage is one of our greatest needs. You need nothing so much as the courage which enables you to stand up to life, come what may. Just to feel the daily daggers of disappointment, physical ailment, thwarted ambitions, financial hardships, and keep on living gallantly, is your greatest need in life.

The encouraging thing is that such courage is not impossible of achievement by you. Where does it come from?

Lions and Tigers

There is hidden deep within each one of us a secret self which is ultimately invincible. This invincible self never gives up the fight. No matter how heavy our burdens, how perplexing our problems, how intense the strain circumstances throw upon us, that inner self never wholly gives way.

Time and again we catch glimpses of it—calm, poised, unafraid. I have stood beside a deathbed and have seen the invincible self fight on long after my friend had lost consciousness. There buried deep in the heart of each of us is that invincible self.

And sometimes we forget that it is there until a crisis comes upon us—and then we make the great discovery. There is something of a hero in each one of us, but it takes adversity, trouble, hardships to bring it out.

During the San Francisco earthquake of 1906 no more heroic work was done for suffering humanity than that done by thieves, gamblers, and harlots. Their heroic selves were there all the time buried underneath the debris of earthiness. It took a crisis to release them.

There is a story that an old Eastern chieftain came to Alexander the Great and presented him with three dogs of ancient lineage and of matchless courage. A few days later Alexander was in a pleasure park, and wishing to amuse himself, had the dogs brought to him.

Having unleashed one, he had a stag released in his presence—but the noble dog looked at the flying stag, yawned, and lay down to sleep. Whereupon Alexander, considering him a useless animal, and not deserving to be fed, had him killed.

He then caused a hind and an antelope to be shown to the other two dogs. But they too, acted just as the first had done. Alexander in anger had them killed also.

The next day, the barbarian chieftain returned to inquire after the health of his favorites. Alexander told him what had happened, adding that he had killed the dogs. Then the chieftain exclaimed:

"O Alexander, you are a great king, but you are a very foolish man. You showed them a stag and an antelope, and they paid no attention—but if you had turned a lion and a tiger loose on them, you would have seen what dogs I had given you!"

Indeed, the invincible self of a man is not awakened by hinds and antelopes—but by lions and tigers. These bring out the character of hidden energies.

The Sword of Faith

When once we recognize the presence of this invincible self, and its power, we begin to understand how God gives us help. The help God gives lies inside our life and not outside.

When we pray, God does not bring about a sudden and miraculous change in the external circumstances of our lives. When we pray earnestly and sincerely, God lifts the bars and sets free that invincible inner self. The release of that inner self, with its superb capacities for endurance and achievement restores our self-confidence, and quickens our courage.

We suddenly realize that even though the odds are heavily against us, we need not go down in pitiful surrender. A new strength, a new resourcefulness, a new wisdom born of desperation, a new determination never to surrender—all these powers emerge within us. The hard situation confronting us may still remain, quite as hard as it was before we prayed, but we ourselves are changed —we become inwardly unconquerable.

Some years ago I conducted the "Week of Spiritual Emphasis" on the campus of a college in Texas. One morning I spoke on the subject "How to Live in a Time of Crisis." Afterward a very humble, quiet little professor of Spanish, took me aside and asked: "Do I look like a man who has just been through a great sorrow?"

"No," I answered, "you certainly do not."

"Well," he said, "my twin daughters, twenty-four years of age, have been in the State Hospital for the Mentally Diseased for three years. I thought that the experience would drive me mad at first, and many nights I walked the streets alone in the snow and cold trying to regain possession of myself. But here I am doing my best to compensate for my loss by giving all the devotion and service I can pour out for my students."

I had already guessed, but I asked the question just the same: "What is the thing that has sustained you through it all?" was the question asked.

Immediately his face became radiant and his eyes sparkled as though suddenly kindled by deep hidden fires: "My Christian Faith," he answered. "Without that I could not have survived."

Christian Faith put a sword in that quiet and lonely man's hand and the courage in his heart to fight against lions and tigers.

Keep a Sturdy Heart

Ezekiel had been a youth in Jerusalem when the Babylonians came down on the city, utterly destroying it and carrying away the most important citizens into exile. As a man he lived a slave amid the oppressive splendor of his conquerors, his own people uprooted, dejected, whipped, and wretched.

And yet in those unfavorable circumstances something happened to Ezekiel that put his name into history. He became one of the major creators of the new Judaism, helping to make possible at last the return from exile, the rebuilding of the temple, the beginning of a new era in man's spiritual life.

What was that something that happened to Ezekiel? Twice in his book he tells us: "The spirit entered into me, and set me on my feet."

It is that assurance of release, of power, of victory in life that makes our religion "Good News!" It is power for life! It gives us courage for life! It sets us on our feet!

When we are convinced beyond the shadow of a doubt that there is a Spirit, call it by whatever name you choose, to back up every noble effort of our lives, then we are encouraged to give ourselves to the highest and holiest tasks—even when defeat seems imminent.

If we are to live both happily and heroically, we must be sustained by a solid confidence, the kind that makes possible spiritual boldness.

Said John Bunyan, when he was under persecution for his religious faith: "If God doth not come, thought I, I will leap off the ladder blindfolded into eternity, sink, swim, come heaven, come hell. Lord Jesus, if Thou will catch me, do, if not, I will venture all for Thy name."

After reaching this momentous decision, frankly facing the fear that God might fail him, and yet daring to make the venture, he experienced the inflow of Divine Power, that mighty force which holds men and women with a tenacious grip and never lets go!

Bunyan could then join the company of the Prophet Ezekiel, who said, when faced by a discouraging experience: "The Spirit entered into me and set me on my feet."

When we dare, as if God is the Reality we believe Him to be, we hear words of assurance like these: "Fear not, for I am with thee, be not dismayed, for I am thy God: I will strengthen thee, I will help thee, I will uphold thee with the right hand of my righteousness."

There is one quotation from the Bible which everyone who would stand up to life unafraid would do well not only to carry with him during the day, but hang on his bedroom wall. There he could look at it every morning before starting out to face the day's struggle. There he could read it every evening, so that it might leaven his subconscious mind as he slept.

That great sentence is this: "In all these things we are more than conquerors through Him that loved us."

Every individual I have ever known who truly practiced the Christian Faith always kept a sturdy heart. I have

(49)

never known a person who believes in and practices—and I would emphasize that word "practices"—sincere faith in God to be defeated.

Such people face life's difficult circumstances, and then go right on singing: "God is our refuge and strength, a very present help in trouble. Therefore will we not fear."

CHAPTER FIVE

DOING SOMETHING ABOUT YOUR FEARS

For a number of years the late Dr. Joseph Fort Newton wrote a newspaper column which was nationally syndicated. He called it "Every Day Religion." The response to his column was tremendous, and each week he received hundreds of letters from his readers, seeking his guidance on all kinds of problems.

From those letters, he said, in which he had an opportunity of "listening in on human lives," he learned many valuable things. After reading piles of letters in which people poured out their souls, some things were burned into his heart, he tells us. The first thing these letters taught him is that Private Enemy No. 1 in human life is neither sin nor sorrow, bad as these can be. Sin can be forgiven and sorrow healed. Nor is it stupidity, since some forms of stupidity can be enlightened. Private Enemy No. 1 is fear, Dr. Newton concluded.

Thus a great, warmhearted man who helped countless thousands of confused individuals to find a new way of life, out of his experience of a long life, reaches out and puts his finger on fear and calls it man's greatest enemy.

It is not too much to say that human life is a battle against fear in which there is no truce. No wonder the French essayist, Montaigne, said, "The thing in the world that I am most afraid of is fear."

No one can be at his best physically, mentally, or

spiritually if he is beset by fears. And God only knows the number of burdened, aching human hearts that would give most anything to be free from the slavery of fear.

Let me note, in passing, that we are not concerned here with the destruction of fear but with its conquest. Fear we cannot destroy, but its conquest is possible. Fear is a native element in human as well as animal life. Fear has been a good thing. It is necessary to survival. Had it not been for fear down through the centuries, you and I would not be here today. Someone has made the comment that fear "does the scouting duty for the fundamental instinct of self-preservation."

The Frog and the Snake

A few summers ago I had the privilege of walking with my six brothers and sister over the old farm in Tennessee where we were reared as youngsters. Though much we remembered has disappeared or changed, there were many spots on that old farm which brought back memories of other days.

There was one place along the little creek bank where I remembered that my father and I surprised a long black snake which had just swallowed a frog. There, about six inches from the snake's mouth, was a big lump, where the frog reposed inside the snake—none too comfortably, you can imagine.

My father, brave soul, caught the snake by its tail and placing one foot behind the lump pulled the snake under his foot, forcing it to disgorge what he had already begun to congratulate himself upon, no doubt, as a tasty dinner. The frog came out leaping and bounding. I have seen a lot of frogs leap in my day, but none like that one. He established some kind of world's record for successive broad jumps as he disappeared in a matter of seconds in the underbrush out of the reach of the snake.

It was fear that enabled that frog to outdo himself that day. It is the frog's fear of the snake that permits it to live to adult froghood and become the father and grandfather of more frogs. If it had no fear, it would only be an item on a reptilian menu, as the frog my father rescued almost became, and in time there would be no more frogs. Baby fowls and animals are taught fear by their parents as soon as they enter this world. It is their only means of assuring their survival.

"There Ain't No Ghosts"

There are numerous ways in which fear works for good in human experience. Fear of pneumonia has kept many a man indoors in bad weather, when that was just where he ought to have been. Dr. E. Stanley Jones said that when one crosses a street where there is heavy traffic he has to make up his mind whether he wants to be numbered among the "quick or the dead." Fear of being run over makes us either quick or careful in traffic. The red light of alarm has kept us from running into physical trouble on the highway of life.

But fear, once essential to life, in the long centuries of evolution, has survived in man in too great an abundance. As his intelligence has developed there has been added another dimension to his world of fear. The animal is frightened only by those things which actually happen, but man with his power of mind can imagine a host of possible or unreal terrors. With his imagination he can look not only into the past but into the future. As a result it is possible for him to keep himself in a constant state of jitters from fear and worry.

Ellis Parker Butler tells the story of a little boy who was

sent by his mother through a graveyard one Halloween night to get a pumpkin for a jack-o'-lantern. There was no moon, it was pitch dark, and the little fellow was scared half to death.

He reached down to pick up what he thought was a pumpkin and a ghost shouted at him: "That's my head!" He was so terrified that the ghost felt sorry for him and said: "Don't you ever be afraid of ghosts, because there ain't no ghosts."

On his way home the little fellow thought it would help a little if he were armed, so he reached down to pick up a stout stick, only to hear another ghost cry out: "That's my leg!" Then a whole company of ghosts materialized, but when they saw how scared he was, they said: "Don't be afraid, there ain't no ghosts."

When he got home and it came time for him to go to bed, he was afraid to go into the dark bedroom. His mother asked: "What are you scared of when there ain't no ghosts?" And the little boy replied: "I ain't scared of the ghosts what am, but I just feel kinda uneasy about the ghosts what ain't."

Well, like the little boy, it's the ghosts "what ain't" that give us the most trouble. Perhaps their most common habitation is in what the psychiatrists call "the anxiety state" of the mind. The person who is afflicted with these ghosts is in a continuous state of fear—physically and mentally. His heart beats wildly, his limbs are weak, he can't digest his food, he sweats easily, and he is short of breath. Aside from all this, he might be classed as a normal person.

Jesus of Nazareth had a lot to say about the kind of fear that is the product of our fancies. He saw that men and women everywhere and at all times have to grapple with fear. He punctuates his speech with such sayings as: "Be not afraid," "Be not anxious," "Fear not." These words

of Jesus show His insight into many a broken and hopeless life.

A *Formula for the Conquest of Fears*

Emerson once said: "He has not learned the lesson of
life who does not every day surmount a fear." But how
are we going to surmount our fears? If we are to live with
a continuous sense of personal power, it is clear that we
must discover ways to conquer our fears.

Basil King in his book *The Conquest of Fear*[1] has given
the world one of the best guides for overcoming fear that
has ever been written. It is the story of his own successful
fight against this great enemy of mankind.

One fall of the year when he was on the borderland
between young manhood and middle life, he found himself in the gardens of the Palace of Versailles face to face
with a dark hour. He was losing his sight. And as an
author, dependent upon voluminous reading, this meant
the probable end of his career. In addition to losing his
sight, he was at odds with his publishers and unable to get
his writings published.

He tells us that he sat in the lonely gardens of the his-
toric French palace amid falling leaves and empty rooms
thinking the whole problem through. He reminds us that
Versailles in autumn is full of sad gardens that stretch into
sad parks, and sad parks into storied and haunting forests,
with châteaux mellowing into ruin. This gloomy setting
seemed to match his mood.

But gradually Basil King worked out this three-point
basis for the conquest of his fears: First of all, he reminded
himself that this is God's world, that He made it and himself and that he was God's agent in the world. He is an

1 Copyright 1921 Doubleday & Company, Inc.

all-sufficient Father, who is all-good. He is Spirit, Love, and Light. Then a verse of scripture leaped into his mind, bringing new life and significance: "Trust in the Lord and do good, and verily thou shalt be fed. Delight thyself in the Lord and He shall give thee the desires of thy heart."

The next thought that came to him was that all men are also God's children and His agents, including his publishers and that he should see them as such. Then this was followed by a third thought: Since these two things are true, all suspicion and fear must go. He resolved to live now as a good son dwelling in the Father's home, for "God is our refuge and strength, a very present help in trouble. Therefore will we not fear, though the earth be removed and though the mountains be carried into the midst of the sea."

That was Basil King's formula for overcoming fear: First of all, he faced it and walked straight toward the thing he feared. Second, he turned the stream of his thought away from self toward God and man, with the confidence that the strength of God was his strength, and that the world of mankind is basically friendly.

The result brought him victory over his fears. Basil King tells us that when he faced the thing he feared and went forward with the confidence that God would give him strength to see him through, things began to change. His blind condition was healed, the difficulty with the publishers evaporated into thin air, and his fear was gone forever.

Here is a formula for you and me as we begin to stagger under the weight of some fear: Stand up and face it and defy it with faith in the power of Almighty God to overcome it then and there or die in the process. It is certain that running away from it will never bring a solution.

One of my fellow ministers tells of being called one day to the bunk house on a Western ranch to comfort a dying cowboy. Sitting beside the bunk the minister tried to divert the sick man's thoughts away from his fear of death by getting him to talk about his life and experiences herding cattle on the plains. "Tell me," the minister said to him, "what important thing have you learned from your experience on the plains that stands out in your memory at this time."

After a few moments of silence the cowboy replied: "The Hereford cows taught me one of life's most important lessons, I reckon. We used to breed cattle for a living, but the severe winter storms used to take an awful toll. Again and again after a severe storm we would find most of them piled up against the fence dead. They would turn their backs to the icy winter blasts and slowly drift downwind twenty miles until the fence stopped them. There they piled up and died.

"But the Herefords were different. They would head straight into the wind and slowly work up the other way until they came to our upper boundary fence where they still stood facing into the storm. We always found them alive and well. That's the greatest lesson I ever learned on these Western prairies."

And so it is when we are assailed by the raging storms of fear. We must take a stand facing the thing we fear, and fight it through to a finish if we are to maintain a wholesome personality.

But it takes more than a brave stand to win out against this fiendish enemy of life. We need a sturdy weapon with which to fight against our stubborn fears. That weapon is faith. The reason so many go down to defeat when they meet fear on the battlefields of life is that we come to the conflict armed with inadequate spiritual resources.

Fear has a way of hypnotizing its victims. It stares us in the face and says to us again and again: "You cannot! You cannot!" And if we listen to it long enough, what it says to us turns out to be true: We cannot. Just as a hypnotist can draw an imaginary line around his victim across which the victim cannot step, just so fear, called by someone "the Svengali of the soul," imprisons us.

It is a terrific experience, and the only way to fight our way out is with the sword of faith. One of the leading psychiatrists of America, speaking out of a long scientific experience, has said: "The only known cure for fear is faith." Faith is creative. It produces what we have faith in. When you live in the depths of your soul by faith, listen to it speaking out of the resources of the Divine world, tap the infinite resources which it can release into your life, then you can win your battle with fear.

The Deep Roots

Recently I read an interesting thing about the hurricane that swept a path of destruction across the New England states in 1938. The trees with shallow roots were torn out of the ground as if they were weeds in a garden. But when the storm had passed some trees remained standing. They were trees with roots which went deep into the earth, so deep that the strongest winds could not dislodge them. Pines and hemlocks and spruces suffered most severely. Their roots were shallow and without the runners which go deep into the earth.

This is a parable of life. People whose spiritual roots are shallow are frequently victims of the storms of fear. But those whose lives drink deeply of the Divine Resources possess a strength beyond their own by which they are able to live triumphantly.

Let me tell you about a man who found this to be true. He is a man with a vital faith in God which shines through his life every day and in every relationship. If you had not known him in other days, you might presume that this atmosphere of triumph is a natural endowment which came with birth, and has remained to add glory to all his life.

But those of us who know him best are aware that it is a quite recent addition to his life. Years before he had come on a period when life was dark. He had been laid off the job he had held for years. His financial condition became quite serious. His wife became ill from worrying over their situation. He himself became ill. They lost their home because payments necessarily ceased on the mortgage.

Worse still, he became afraid. Fear kept him tossing each night through many hours of wakefulness. Fear made it difficult for him to eat. It threatened his life.

One Sunday night, he says, he lay awake thinking over the message he had heard at his church that morning. At the time he was listening to it, there seemed to be nothing exceptional about it. But now he whispered aloud a verse of scripture the minister quoted in his sermon: "I can do all things through Him who gives me strength."

He repeated it several times. "I can do all things"—that means all the things he feared, he told himself. "Through Him"—that means Divine power. "Who gives me strength" —that means something personal.

In telling his minister about his experience, he said that he told himself: "Why that verse of scripture has my name on it! It is especially for me!" And then, a Presence seemed to enter his life at that moment. From that hour on he has been a transformed individual. No more fears, no more anxieties. Life became different for him. He had discovered that God gives us "the spirit of power" as a substitute for fear.

Whatever problem you face, whatever evil stares you in the face, whispering, "You cannot win!" there is another —a still small voice speaking to you, if you will but listen —saying: "You can win! You can do what you ought to do.

You can stand what you must endure. 'As your day is so shall your strength be.' And however difficult the circumstances, you can have an inner victory, the conquest of panic and fear—for you 'can do all things through Him who gives you strength.'"

CHAPTER SIX

LEARNING TO HANDLE LIFE'S INTERRUPTIONS

Life is full of interruptions. Interruptions, great and small, significant, and insignificant, come almost daily.

How many homes know what it means to have the even flow of life interrupted by someone in that home being called into the service of the armed forces. How many well-laid plans for education, marriage, and jobs have been delayed.

Sudden illness comes to someone, and without warning, ordered family life must give way to emergency measures. When tragedy comes, breaking into the pleasant and convenient routines of daily living, it always means readjustment and redirection of life.

There are minor obligations which unexpectedly and persistently call for our attention, even when we would much rather not be bothered.

Life's interruptions are inevitable. How to handle them in such a way that we make the most of them is a common problem.

The Blessing of Interruptions

Ofttimes the interruptions which come to us in life bring blessings without measure.

Once I was late for an appointment and was driving as fast as the speed limit would allow—and then some, I suspect—when I saw just ahead of me a street blockade.

Workmen were repairing the pavement in the block ahead. Of course there was the familiar arrow pointing at right angles to the street with the word DETOUR.

My first reaction was one of irritation, but I quickly recovered my poise and decided that since I was going to have to take the detour, whether I liked it or not, I might as well enjoy it. I began looking for interesting things I would have missed had I not been detoured. And sure enough, there were a lot of them.

First of all, I found myself on a street I had not been on before. It was a beautiful street, lined with stately trees and attractive houses. A most unusual front fence caught my attention, and in the corner of a yard I saw a gorgeous red rose bush.

A little farther on I heard from somewhere the most heavenly music this world knows—the joyous laughter of a little child. I passed two schools and saw the young people playing and heard them bantering with each other. At one street corner I saw strolling along on the sidewalk an aged Oriental woman with the shining face of a saint.

All this I saw, and more, on my detour, which enriched the rest of my day. In fact, I was so absorbed in the enjoyment of my interrupted journey that I almost bumped into the rear of a car in front of me. Had I done so, I would have no doubt experienced an interesting interruption within my interruption—but not one I would have enjoyed.

What a parable of life was my experience! How many times larger and more serious interruptions in life bring unanticipated blessings, if accepted in the right spirit.

Do you remember what happened to Conrad the cobbler? Edwin Markham tells us about him in his poem "How the Great Guest Came."[1]

[1] Edwin Markham, *Shoes of Happiness* (Doubleday & Company, Inc., 1915).

Learning to Handle Life's Interruptions

The Lord came to him in a vision and promised that He would visit his shop on a certain day. And throughout that day Conrad anticipated the fulfillment of the Lord's promise. But the Lord did not visit him.

A weary beggar, a hungry woman, and a homeless child came to his door. To each he willingly gave of what he had and according to the need. But his Lord came not.

In the dusk of the evening, Conrad sat in quiet reverie in his shop, disappointed that the Lord had not visited him that day. As he pondered over the meaning of his vision, he heard again the Voice, which assured him that the Lord had kept His promise and had visited the cobbler three times during the day: He was the beggar, the woman, and the child who came to the door of the shop asking for help, which Conrad had gladly given.

Sometimes we not only entertain angels unaware, but even God Himself—and He comes to us many times in life's unwelcome interruptions.

One of America's prized literary masterpieces was made possible by an interruption that lasted twenty-five years! The book is Oliver Wendell Holmes' *The Autocrat of the Breakfast Table*. He began the book with the words: "I was just going to say, when I was interrupted." The interruption referred to in that opening sentence was (Dr. Holmes tells us in the introduction) just a quarter of a century in duration.

But if the interruption had never occurred, and if the book had been written when it was first commenced, it is certain that *The Autocrat of the Breakfast Table* would not have turned out to be the book we all treasure so highly and love so much. His wise reflections on life came as a result of the rich experiences which he accumulated during the twenty-five years of living and observing human life.

How many of the books now flooding the market—perhaps even this one—would have been increased in value if they had come out of a similar interruption.

How shall we handle the interruptions we encounter in life, so that we may make the most of them? It is my conviction that we shall do so by recognizing three simple principles.

The first one is to accept interruptions as a part of life. We must force ourselves to stop fighting against unwelcome interruptions to the even flow of life, and surrender quietly to them.

Only as we yield to the situations which we find ourselves powerless to change, can we free ourselves from fatal inward tensions. Only so can we acquire the inward quietness amid which we can seek—and usually find—ways by which our interruptions can be made at least endurable.

To accept the interruptions we are powerless to change, accept them permanently, as well as provisionally, accept them hopefully rather than despairingly, accept them positively instead of negatively—to do this is to take the first step on the long, hard road of an adequate personal adjustment to life.

Three Simple Principles

Why is it so difficult for some people to accept interruptions as a part of life? Isn't it because most of us were told in childhood that the way to conquer a difficulty is to fight it and demolish it?

That theory is, of course, the one that should be taught to young people. Many of the difficulties we encounter in youth are not permanent. And the combination of a heroic courage, a resolute will, and a tireless persistence will often—probably usually—break them down.

But in later years the essential elements in the situation change. We find in our little world prison walls which no amount of battering will demolish. Within those walls we must spend our days—spend them happily or resentfully.

Under these circumstances we must deliberately reverse our youthful technique. We must gain victory, not be assaulting the walls, but by accepting them, and learning to live within them. Only when this surrender is made can we assure ourselves of inward quietness, and locate the next step on the road to ultimate victory.

❈   ❈   ❈

In the second place, if we are going to be successful in handling the interruptions that break into our lives, we should keep in mind that many an interruption has proved to be a blessing rather than an evil.

No one in our generation can think about the interruptions of life without calling to mind the many young men who went off to military service during World War II. At the time, being called into the service just at the crucial time in their lives when they were starting into business, or were completing their education, or had plans to marry and establish a home must have seemed to them a cruel act of fate.

But in these later years many of them have had reasons to be grateful for the interruption. While in the service of their country some of them made lasting friendships with some of the men they met. Some of them, like many young men I know, were stationed in places where they met the girls whom they later married and with whom they are now enjoying a happy family life. Their interruption turned out to be a blessing in disguise.

John Bunyan was an itinerant English tinker and a preacher. Some of the things he said offended the civil authorities and he was thrown into jail. How that interruption of his work must have galled him at first! But he made use of his time while in jail to write one of our greatest English classics, *Pilgrim's Progress*.

* * *

In the third place, disappointment, change of plans, or other interruptions, are often the golden gates to a more glorious life of service to others and of service to those larger purposes which routine living may not bring.

One of the greatest benefactors of Japan was a man by the name of Alpheus Hardy. And it came about as the result of an interruption in his life.

He was not a college man, and it was the bitter disappointment of his life that he could not be one. His earliest ambition was to go to college and become a minister. So he enrolled in Phillips Academy to prepare himself.

His health broke down, and, in spite of his determined hope of being able to go on, at last the truth was forced upon him that he could not. How deep was his disappointment! It seemed as if all his hopes and purposes in life had been defeated. He said that the anguished thought that kept going through his mind was, "I cannot be God's minister!"

When at last that fact became certain to him, one morning alone in his room, his distress was so great that he threw himself flat on the floor. The voiceless cry of his soul, he said, was: "O God, I cannot be Thy minister!"

Then there came to him, as he lay on the floor, a vision, a new hope, a perception that he could serve God in business with the same devotion as in preaching, and that to make money for God might be his sacred calling. The vision of this service, and its nature were so clear and joyous that he arose to his feet with new hope in his heart.

He exclaimed aloud: "O God, I can be Thy minister! I

will go back to Boston. I will make money for God, and that shall be my ministry!"

From that time on he felt himself as much appointed and ordained to make money for God, as if he had been permitted to carry out his own plans and been ordained to preach. The ministry to which he was called, he was convinced, was to make and administer money for God.

He felt that his life had been interrupted, but he determined to make the interruption like the pause in the music—that adds effectiveness to all that goes before it and impressiveness to all that follows after.

Then comes the romantic sequel. Alpheus Hardy came in course of time to own a line of steamers that traded with Japan. On one of them a little Japanese boy stowed away, and when the ship arrived in Boston, the captain brought him to Mr. Hardy.

Mr. Hardy talked kindly to the boy, prayed with him, pointed out to him the Christian way of life, and gave him a first-class university education. Then young Neesima went back to Japan to spread the Christian faith from one end of the empire to the other. No name in the annals of Japan is more honored than is his.

Had Alpheus Hardy achieved his heart's desire and been a minister, it is exceedingly problematical as to whether he could ever have accomplished so fine a work as that. The interruption of his well-laid plans for his future life opened for him a golden gate for a much richer life of service than he ever dreamed for himself.

The Interruption We Call Death

And what shall we say of life's greatest and most disturbing interruption of all—one that none escapes—the interruption of our earthly existence, which we call death. Can we not also apply the three principles we have mentioned to this experience? Death should be accepted, without rebellion, as a part of life; it should be looked upon as nothing more than an interruption; and it should be recognized as the golden gate to a more glorious life.

Is it not conceivable that the first words that most of us will utter on the other side of the grave will be those with which Oliver Wendell Holmes begins his book? "I was just going to say, when I was interrupted,". Life, like the parts of a serial story, is always "to be continued."

"I feel," wrote Victor Hugo, "that I have not said a thousandth part of what is in me. When I go down to the grave I shall have ended my day's work. But another day will begin next morning. Life closes in the twilight, it opens with the dawn."

It is our Christian faith that, when we resume our old relationships beyond death and take up our tasks anew, we shall find that those fine friendships will have been sweetened and those hallowed activities perfected by the temporary break.

Then we shall comprehend that, which is now beyond our finite understanding, that life as a whole has been immeasurably enriched by the interruption.

CHAPTER SEVEN

STANDING UP TO LIFE UNDER PRESSURE

Sometimes a return to the original language in which the New Testament was written gives new insight into some of its passages. For instance, there are those words which Jesus spoke just before he experienced the agony of the Garden of Gethsemane: "In the world you will have tribulation." What is the meaning of the word tribulation?

A study of the word in the original Greek is quite revealing. The Greeks had a verb which means "to press" or "to squeeze." They used it to describe, for example, what happens when a crowd closes in on some individual. He is pressed, or squeezed by the crowd. That is the literal meaning of the Greek verb.

But the verb is also used in a figurative sense— "to afflict," or "to bring tribulation upon." Therefore, when the crowd closes in on one, it afflicts him or brings tribulation upon him.

From this verb came a noun whose literal meaning is "pressure," and whose figurative meaning is "affliction" or "tribulation." This noun is the one used in the 16th chapter of John where Jesus is quoted as saying: "In the world you will have tribulation."

But suppose we give the Greek noun its literal rather than its figurative meaning. Then we should translate it thus: "In the world you will have pressure."

I don't know what the disciples thought about the truth

(69)

of those words of the Master. But one doesn't have to convince us twentieth-century folk that pressure is what we have the most of in our day. We live in a day when terrific forces press us from without and from within.

As our modern living becomes more intricate and involved it gathers weight and speed until it seems like a monster we have created but can't control. Everywhere the tension tightens. In every trade, business and professional men have to go at a killing pace to do what is expected of them. Life becomes so filled with anxiety that the big question is not so much how to succeed as how to keep one's soul alive.

Ours is a jumpy, jerky, dizzy age—ever shifting like a spotlight and we live in a hurrying day-by-dayness. No wonder the meaning of life is blurred in the scramble for the means of living, and the still small voice of moral integrity is so often drowned in the pell-mell medley of chattering events.

We cannot escape the pressures of modern life, so our problem is how to meet it and not be crushed by it. How can we live in a troubled, hard-driving world with quietness and confidence?

Once a congressman was reporting to an audience of his constituents the reason for his questionable vote on a certain measure before Congress. "You can't imagine," he said, "the terrific pressure that is brought to bear upon your congressmen." An old retired sea captain, who had brought his ship safely to port through many a howling storm, yelled at the congressman: "But man, what about your inner braces?"

How necessary it is for us to give attention to our "inner braces" if we are to withstand the pressures of life without being crushed by them.

Take Time to Relax

First of all, we need to give more time and attention to mental relaxation.

High tension is a prevailing American malady. The adult who has not watched apprehensively the doctor take his blood pressure is in the minority. Apparently Americans have always been more or less of this tense type.

I was reading recently of a French writer who came to this country in 1830 to study the American, whom he classified as "a new breed of man on the earth." The French visitor noted the restless aggressiveness of our people. "The American," he complained, "is so restless that he has even invented a chair, called a rocking chair, in which he can move while he sits."

If this French observer could see us now, he would be forced to revise upward his conclusions, as the tempo has mounted.

A careful and consistent cultivation of a relaxed mental attitude is important in reducing tension. Athletes know that trying too hard throws them off their timing.

A number of years ago I had frequent conversations with a man who had coached several championship basketball teams. He told me that he attributed his success to the fact that he was able to teach his players how to relax.

He even wrote a book on the art of relaxation, the manuscript of which he showed me before its publication. Out of his experience, he told me, he had discovered that the fine coordination which characterizes the great men of sport is attained by the principle of "taking the game in stride, remembering that 'easy does it.'"

"Or if you prefer a scripture passage," he said, "to an

athletic expression, you can take this one from Isaiah: 'In quietness and confidence shall be your strength.' "

Develop Vision

But we need something more than just to relax the mind, if we are going to withstand the devastating pressures of our fast moving days. We need to fill our minds with something other than the cares and worries and anxieties of daily living. We need to give more attention to the life of the intellect.

We must cultivate a wide and quiet place of vision, a place of vantage, from which to see life in the large and in long perspective, if we are not to be confused and overwhelmed by it. It is true, as Isaiah says, that we must have mental relaxation, "that in quietness and confidence shall be thy strength." But if one has only quietness and confidence in his mind there is danger it might become nothing more than a vacuum.

Something more is needed, and one of the Proverbs has the answer: "Where there is no vision, [the] people perish."

Every day teaches me the necessity—not the mere luxury—of communion with the master spirits of the race, as essential to the health and sanity of our lives. Three things the great masters of literature have to give us: serenity, vision, and beauty. And the greatest of these is vision —without which the world within the mind is an unlit chaos, and the world without, a wild bedlam.

Books of the day come and go, leaving hardly a trace behind, giving us only passing thoughts of things eternal. But the great books lift us on the wings of vision to the mountaintops. They see what other men only look at. They kindle the mind and warm the heart, they give us a background against which to interpret the pageant of affairs.

They cast over the tide of passing events the light of spiritual insight and moral values, by which we may correct our estimates and renew our faith in the "ultimate decency of things." By helping us see life steadily and see it whole, they reveal the eternal in the midst of time, and rescue us from cynicism and pessimism to which we are tempted.

During the many hours I spent wandering through Westminster Abbey in London, I was deeply impressed —as another American traveler, Washington Irving, a century and a half ago, said he was impressed—by the fact that more people lingered in the Poets' Corner of the famous Abbey than at any other place.

It was nothing more than curiosity that caused visitors to the Abbey, including myself, to walk by and take a brief look at the tombs of the kings and queens—Henry VII, Edward the Confessor, Queen Elizabeth I, Mary Queen of Scots, and many others. They took even less time before the monuments of statesmen, admirals, and generals.

But people not only stop and look at the simple monuments and marble slabs covering the earthly remains of the men who have left us a heritage of books; they linger for some time as if in silent tribute to departed friends. For as Washington Irving tells us, when the visitor turns from the tombs and monuments of the kings and queens, the statesmen, the admirals and the generals, and enters the Poets' Corner:

"A kinder and fonder feeling takes place of that cold curiosity or vague admiration with which they gaze on the splendid monuments of the great and heroic. They linger about these as about the tombs of friends and companions, for indeed there is something of companionship between the author and the reader.

"Other men are known to posterity only through the medium of history, which is continually growing faint and obscure, but the intercourse between the author and his fellow-men is ever new, active and immediate.

"He has lived for them more than for himself, he has sacrificed surrounding enjoyments, and shut himself up from the delights of social life, that he might the more intimately commune with distant minds and distant ages . . .

"Well may posterity be grateful to his memory, for he has left it an inheritance, not of empty names and sounding actions, but whole treasures of wisdom, bright gems of thought, and golden veins of language."[1]

To take from the bookshelf one of these friends, and listen attentively to his words of wisdom and insight sends us back to master life and not be mastered by it.

It was in an hour of great need that I discovered Ralph Waldo Emerson. It was in one of those times when the high pressures of life had forced me into a corner, and seemed to be moving in for the final "knock-out," to use an expression borrowed from the prize fight ring. It was while taking advantage of a quiet moment, between "rounds," that I took from the bookshelf a copy of Emerson's essays and turned to the one on "Self-Reliance." Then I read the one on "The Oversoul," and "History."

No words of mine can ever tell the debt I owe the Sage of Concord, whose serene and luminous spirit touched me when it was most needed, and has helped me through the intervening years. He helped me to see life and believe in it, to put my trust in God and not be afraid of life. Years

[1] Washington Irving, *The Sketch Book* (New York: G. P. Putnam's Sons, 1880).

have come and gone, but that day I became acquainted with Emerson is fresh and vivid in my memory.

You must or have already made your own discovery of the writer or perhaps the artist or musician who has kindled your mind and spirit, and helped you meet life with courage and serenity, in spite of outward pressures.

Great writers, artists, and musicians help us to the nobler mood, the clearer insight, the broader outlook. We owe it to ourselves to make their acquaintance. If we give them the opportunity, they can redeem us from the mental stress and strain of the world, and help us find meaning in the midst of life's pressures.

The Rest Jesus Promised

However, if one is to stand up to life under its pressures, he must not only have special times of mental relaxation, and of intellectual inspiration, but above all he must learn to go about his work and live his life without mental and emotional strain.

Once Jesus stopped in the midst of His prayer and said: "Come to me, all who labor and are heavy-laden, and I will give you rest." I do not think the Master meant that He would give us rest from toil but teach us how to rest as we toil. And the thing He has to teach us is how to practice the presence of God in the midst of life's pressures.

At a certain spot along Aldersgate Street in London there once stood a little Moravian Chapel. The building has long since been torn down, but a plaque commemorates the place where it stood. That little chapel is remembered as the place where John Wesley was converted one night at a Moravian prayer meeting.

As I stood there I found myself reflecting upon the career of the remarkable man. Perhaps no business executive of our modern day works under more pressure than did John Wesley during the eighteenth century. The last fifty years of his life were the most strenuous years any man in history ever lived.

During that time he preached over 40,000 times, an average of about fifteen sermons a week. It is estimated that he traveled more than 250,000 miles up and down and across the British Isles. He crossed the English Channel to Ireland more than fifty times. He preached in fishing villages in Cornwall, isolated mining towns in Yorkshire, where the regular highways never reached.

Up to 1773 when he was seventy years of age all of John Wesley's land journeys were done on horseback. He wrote a number of books and organized and started on its distinguished career the great Methodist Church. He died in 1791 at the age of eighty-seven, active and alert until the very end.

What did such a super-strenuous career do to this energetic little man who was only five feet four inches tall and weighed less than 125 pounds? Did it leave him a physical and nervous wreck? To a remarkable degree Wesley retained almost to the end of his long life, full vigor of mind and body.

What was the secret of Wesley's power to stand up to life and maintain his health and sanity under tremendous pressure? Behind the mighty achievements of his life, we catch a glimpse of a man whose inner life was unusually confident, and free from tension. It was this emotional poise which was the ultimate source of his ability to shoulder a multitude of burdens.

Just as his busy life was beginning, John Wesley expressed in verse that state of mind which for the last fifty years of his life was to enable him to live a life of calm in the midst of strenuous days. It is a message that we in this high-pressure day need:

Commit thou all thy griefs
And ways into God's hands,
To His sure truth and tender care
Who heaven and earth commands.

Who points the clouds their course,
Whom winds and seas obey,
He shall direct thy wandering feet,
He shall prepare the way.

No profit canst thou gain
From self-consuming care!
To God commend thy cause! His ear
Attends thy softest prayer.

Those words were set to music and sung as a hymn in the early Methodist Churches, and one can almost imagine he can hear Wesley singing it as he rode on his long, lonely journeys on horseback across the lovely English countryside.

That hymn of Wesley's reveals the secret of his power. His inner life was at rest, while his outer life was under pressure.

He had learned that most priceless lesson which the prophet Isaiah learned long ago, and which we must learn today, if we are to stand up to life's pressures: "Thou shalt keep him in perfect peace, whose mind is stayed on Thee."

CHAPTER EIGHT

WHEN THE ROAD GETS SLIPPERY

No drama in the history of the world's literature compares with the Book of Job. The name of the playwright has been lost in the mists of antiquity, but the greatness of the drama remains. It has everything which great drama requires, but above all it has a great theme: the problem of evil.

The author of the Book of Job, contrary to the popular belief of the time, saw that evil is no respecter of persons. Evil attacks both good men and bad men. Thus, when he wanted to portray the direst visitation of evil, he selected as the victim a good man named Job.

In a contest between God and Satan, all kind of evil things are visited upon Job. His property was destroyed, his sons and daughters die, and he himself was stricken with a painful disease. So the story begins.

Job groaning in his distress is visited by three of his friends. In their efforts to console him they argue, as many people nowadays do, that Job had committed some dreadful sin for which God is punishing him. Job strongly maintains they are mistaken. The stalwart character of Job is revealed in an unexpected place in the dialogue with his friend Eliphaz. In the midst of his accusations Eliphaz says one thing about Job which throws more light on his character than any other thing said about him.

Remembering the years when Job was in his prime, a

helper and encourager of his people, Eliphaz said to him: "Your words have kept men on their feet and have nerved the weak."

Men who can do that are always in demand. Certainly we need those who can speak such words to us living in this age. It is a slippery road over which we travel today—both collectively and individually—and sometimes we have trouble keeping on our feet. There come times in the experience of each of us when "we can not go on unless we can hold on." When the road gets slippery, we need someone to speak the words that will keep us on our feet. For there is no questioning the power of a word fitly spoken to one in need.

In *My Fair Lady*, Eliza Doolittle interrupts her ardent suitor in the midst of his passionate profession of love by exclaiming, "Words, words, words, I'm so sick of words . . . If you're in love, show me!"

Now there are times when most of us become impatient with words where we think the situation calls for action. But sometimes the strongest foundation that can be put under a human life is the most intangible thing we can deal with—a word. The writer of Proverbs is right when he says: "A word spoken in due season, how good it is!" And again: "A word fitly spoken is like apples of gold in pictures of silver."

A word can sometimes do harm, but we are concerned here with the good they can accomplish when spoken by people with the spirit of Job. "Your words have kept men on their feet," Eliphaz tells him. People live by words, for words are creative when properly spoken.

Words Fitly Spoken

Sometimes a few words of encouragement can keep one on his feet when his road becomes slippery from the heavy rains of despair.

When the Road Gets Slippery

A number of years ago a bookkeeper in one of our large cities committed suicide. He left a note behind which read as follows: *"I have been a member of this firm for twenty years. In every way I have tried to be loyal to it. I have given my best years to its service. Yet in all those twenty years I have never received one word of praise, or appreciation. I can't stand it any longer."*

Perhaps someone will claim that those are the words of a weakling and a coward. Not necessarily. That man failed to receive from someone what he had every right as a human being to expect—the encouragement of his superiors and associates. He needed someone with the heart of Job to speak a word to him that would keep him on his feet when his road became slippery with the mud of despair.

A few years ago I saw a motion picture called *The Red Shoes*. Many critics proclaimed it one of the greater motion pictures. The story is based on one of those charming tales of Hans Christian Andersen.

For more than a century and a half parents the world over have been reading to their children the immortal fairy tales of Andersen. It has been estimated that next to the New Testament no books have done more than his to teach love on earth. But the genius of Andersen, during his early years, came close to being blasted by discouragement.

He was born in poverty, his grandfather died insane. He wanted to be an actor, but they said that he was too ugly. He believed that he could write, but in school his teachers, seeing him with his pen in hand, used to say: "What rot are you slinging together now?" With his teachers pouring scorn upon his abilities, Andersen with his soul scarred deep wrote the words in his diary: *"Blame dulls me, praise gives me courage—it makes me cling to God."*

Finally, one of Andersen's stories found a publisher, and he took it with him to Jonas Collin, one of the counselors of the King of Denmark. That call was the turning point in his life. The words of recommendation to the king and later words of encouragement to young Hans Christian Andersen set the young man on his feet, and he went on to become the world's greatest writer of fairy tales.

Jonas Collin was a man with the heart of Job, his words kept a young man on his feet when his road had become slippery with discouragement.

There is a charming ancient Grecian legend which tells of the man who, having a deep affection for the young, used to hide himself in the bushes along the road that led to the temple. Whenever he saw a tired child loitering or faltering on the sacred path, he would roll a golden ball in front of the halting youth. The ball would make the youth forget his fatigue, and his feet once more would hasten on toward the temple.

How like "a word fitly spoken" to someone who has found the road he travels difficult! It is like a golden ball of hope. There are some great time-honored words which, spoken in due season, have kept men and women on their feet, when their road through life has become slippery and uncertain underfoot.

Honor

One of these great words is "Honor."

A young man approached the challenging adventure of adulthood with the serious intention of making a success of his life. He started out to interview a selected group of successful men in various careers. He went to a famous writer and said: "Sir, you have written much for a great many men. Will you write something especially for me?

I want one word which I may hold in my heart as though it were the most priceless jewel of life—one word from you to me that will always be the touchstone of my life." And this is what the great man wrote for him: "Honor!"

One of the greatest men I knew in my youth—or for that matter, during my lifetime—died not long ago in Nashville, Tennessee. He was the headmaster of the little preparatory school I attended as a boy. Like the hundreds of other boys who came under his influence, I owe more to him than any other man next to my father.

It was this man who encouraged me, five brothers and a sister to lay a solid foundation for an education. The little preparatory school was forced to close its doors about thirty years ago, because of financial difficulties, and its buildings have long since either been torn down or converted to other uses. But the influence of James A. Robins, whom his students affectionately called "Mr. Jim," will never die.

The one word in his vocabulary, the one he sought to stamp indelibly upon our minds, was the one word, "Honor." Wherever they were to go in life, he urged them to let that one word wave like a banner at the masthead of their ship of character.

Before every examination, every athletic contest, or any other experience where character would be put to the test, we can never forget the way he recited with emphasis some lines from Robert Burns. So many times did we hear him recite those words that I am sure his students wherever they are at the present time can still remember them, and the one who reminded us of them. There is little wonder, therefore, that years later when I found myself standing beside the grave of Robert Burns in Dumfries, Scotland, the poets words recited by my old teacher came back to me:

The fear of hell's the hangman's whip
To hold the wretch in order,
But where you feel your honor grip,
Let that be your border.

Not once, but times without number, "Mr. Jim" told us: "When one loses his honor, he has lost everything worth holding to. It is the very bedrock of our social structure and of western civilization." And many a time when the road has become slippery, "Mr. Jim" has been a Job to me, speaking the word that has kept me on my feet. And that word is "Honor!"

Courage

Another word which spoken in due season has a way of keeping men on their feet is "Courage."

Winston Churchill has said: "Courage is the first of human qualities, because it is the one quality which guarantees all the others." With courage gone, no character can long survive. But with it, defeat and destruction cannot overwhelm us.

When William Faulkner received the Nobel Prize for his work in literature in Stockholm, Sweden, several years ago, he made a memorable speech. He used the moment of his great triumph as a platform from which to speak to the young men and women who would come after him in the field of literature. "Among these," he said, "is already that one who will some day stand where I am now standing." Listen to Mr. Faulkner:

"Our tragedy today is a general and universal fear, so long sustained by now that we can even bear it. . . . He [the writer] must teach himself that the basest of all things is to be afraid."

Although William Faulkner was delivering a message to

his young fellow writers, it is a message for each of us today. His words are like a cool breeze blowing through the corridors of our modern life, that are heavy with the rancid air of pessimism, despair, and hopelessness. We are being bombarded from all sides with gospels of doom. Disheartening predictions of disaster are being hurled at us from our military men, our government officials, from the press, the radio and television, from the platform and from the pulpit.

I would not minimize for one moment the seriousness of our present problems—at home or on the world-wide scene. There is seething unrest throughout the world. But if we expect to preserve our stability, we had better remember the words of William Faulkner and heed them: "The basest of all things is to be afraid." We must not cringe in fear before our contemporary problems. That way lies defeat. Only a great courage can sustain us as we face our present problems.

One of the first things that ought to be said to one upon whom has come some great overwhelming tragic experience is "Keep up your courage!" A man said to me not long ago: "Perhaps you do not remember saying it, but once when I was going through one of the most trying periods of my life, you grasped my hand and said: 'Keep your chin up!' You will never know how much those four words spoken by you in my time of need helped me to pull myself together and face what I had to face with courage."

I was grateful to know that I had been a Job to my friend in his time of need, and had spoken a word of courage that had helped him stay on his feet.

Belief

But one of the grandest words in our vocabulary to keep us on our feet when the road gets slippery is the word "Believe!"

How many people waver and inwardly die because their capacity to believe in anything that has meaning and worth dies, and doubt arises, mistrust comes forth, and suspicion stalks about. Doubt of self, doubt of friends, doubt of the world, doubt of justice, doubt of causes to which one once committed himself, doubt of God, doubt of life itself—which is another way of saying "a living death."

I read a poem years ago concerning a group of men seated upon the shore of a desert island where they had been cast following a shipwreck. There in that lonely place each one recounted the losses he had sustained, not as a result of the shipwreck but before the disaster—the far more disastrous losses in life itself. One spoke of the loss of a happy home, another of the loss of some loved one. Still others spoke of the losses of business, reputation, money, or fame.

The last to speak summed up his loss in these tragic lines: "Great losses have ye met, but mine is heavier yet: For the believing heart has gone from me." When one suffers the tragic loss of the believing heart, then honor, courage, and the rest of the qualities that make for great living cannot sustain one for long.

It is little short of amazing to discover what magic there is in believing. It gathers up one's life and pulls it together, and gives it direction, as nothing else can do. It sets goals and then marshals intelligence and energy to achieve them. It releases power when all other devices fail. What magic there is in believing!

When the Road Gets Slippery

At one time in my youth I had an ambition to become a professional magician. I even went so far in that direction as to appear in public performances, assisted by my younger brother, Rex, who in addition to being Superintendent of Schools in Ada, Oklahoma, at the present time is still a magician of no mean ability. In those days of my youth I read every book on magic I could lay my hands on, even the lives of some of the great performers of the art, such as Herman the Great, Harry Keller, Houdini, Blackstone, and Cardini.

However, my great hero was Howard Thurston. He was the one I most earnestly wanted to emulate. I saw him perform on one or two occasions. I read his autobiography *My Life of Magic* in which he tells not only of his experiences on the stage but of his early struggles against poverty. He seemed to have been born with a burning ambition to be a magician, along with an unshakable belief in himself and his ability to reach his goal.

As a boy he ran away from home and made his way to Chicago, where he supported himself as a newsboy. One cold winter night in 1884, Thurston tells us, he was standing in the alley between the Chicago Tribune Building and the old McVicker's Theatre. He stood there watching the well-dressed crowd of people leaving the famous theatre. He vowed to himself then and there that someday he was going to present a show in that same theatre.

While waiting for the last edition of the Chicago *Tribune* to come off the press, this little ragged newsboy walked across the alley to the theatre side. And, as if to impress his vow upon his mind lest he forget it, he took his knife and scratched his initials "H.T." in one of the bricks in the wall of the theatre.

That night as usual, after selling his papers, young Thurston returned to the alley, cold and hungry, wrapped himself in some newspapers and went to sleep on the iron grating beside the Tribune Building. The warm air from the press room in the basement below kept him from freezing.

Twenty-three years later, Howard Thurston did present a show in the McVicker's Theatre, where he was billed as the world's greatest magician. Between acts, he led one of his fellow magicians out into the alley, and there on the wall in one of the bricks he pointed to the dim marks of his initials made there almost a quarter of a century before.

Howard Thurston during his lifetime performed on the theatre stages around the world amazing feats of magic. But none of his stage magic could compare with the magic of believing in himself and his destiny which could transform a ragged newsboy into a world-renowned entertainer in twenty-three years.

The magic of believing, as Claude M. Bristol has told us, is the most wonderful magic in all the world! God has so created us that the mastery of life comes from within. When we recognize, come to terms with, and use this magic capacity of believing which God has placed within us, we achieve inner power, self-assurance, poise, and the confidence that enables us to handle life.

How we need some Job to keep us on our feet by saying to us that which Jesus once said to a man who brought his son to the Master to be healed: "All things are possible to him who believes."

Could it not have been words such as these—honor, courage, and belief—which Eliphaz had in mind when he said of Job: "Your words have kept men on their feet and have nerved the weak"? If so, are there any greater words for us to keep us on our feet when we come to those slippery places along the road of life?

And there are no greater words we can give to others!

CHAPTER NINE

A QUIET MIND IN AN UNQUIET WORLD

Our age has been called by many names, such as "The Power Age," "The Atomic Age," and "The Space Age."

Someone has even called it "The Aspirin Age," and has tried to estimate the number of tons of aspirin and sedatives consumed by the American people in a year's time. Next to beer and used cars, the sedative industry sponsors more TV and radio programs than any other product.

One writer refers to our age as "The Ulcer Age." The ulcer has become a kind of badge of success, he contends.

Somewhere I saw a cartoon, picturing an American businessman with three telephones on his desk, all ringing at once, while the businessman, with a cigar in his mouth, is dictating a telegram to one secretary, while dictating a letter to another secretary—and two of his junior partners are waiting while he completes a long-distance call. And under the picture was the one word: "Success."

Ours is an "Age of the Jitters," someone else says, and adds that if we have a patron saint it must be "St. Vitus."

Recently I received an autographed copy of the latest book of a friend of mine, Stella Terrill Mann, entitled *How to Analyze and Overcome Your Fears.*[1] She calls our age, "The Age of Fear."

Whatever our age is called, certainly we hardly need

[1] New York: Dodd, Mead & Co., 1962.

(89)

the poet W. H. Auden to tell us that this age might well be called "The Age of Anxiety." We have only to look at the faces of our fellows in their offices, on the streets, or wherever we meet them, to see the tell-tale evidences of nervous strain, and frequently the fear and worry which so often accompanies it.

Many people, perhaps most people, never learn how to manage anxiety. Throughout life they are burdened, perplexed, overwrought.

Almost never do they escape from the shadows, and make their way into the sunshine. Always the unquietness of the world about them invades their inner world and keeps them from relaxing with a quiet mind.

If one could roll up his sleeves, clench his fists, grit his teeth, and with one mighty surging of his will put an end to all anxiety, many more of us than now do could relax into serenity and confidence. Overcoming an anxiety is more than a matter of willpower, the problem goes deeper than that.

Anxiety is but the symptom of a sickly way of life. We need more than a little salve on the outside to clear up the complexion of our outlook. We need spiritual vitamins, so that ability to deal with the often tragic concerns of life comes from an inner radiance, a serene and confident interior strength.

I like Goodspeed's translation of the words of Jesus, when he says: "Do not worry about life." Jesus in his teachings insists that we can be free from anxiety.

But how can we achieve a quiet mind in an unquiet world?

Practice Mental Peace

First, one has to practice a new attitude of mind.

You will notice that I use the word "practice," because

the art of handling our anxieties and achieving a quiet mind cannot be developed all at once.

A young violin player cannot have an instrument placed in his hands and play Schubert's "Serenade" in a few days. An awkward country boy cannot be made into a polished athlete with a few days' practice.

Neither can one give up his anxieties, his worries and his fears, and develop a quiet attitude toward life by a wave of the hand and a wish that it be so. It takes practice.

As a matter of fact, the person who becomes a chronic worrier gets that way through practice. The most successful worriers that I know—and I know a lot of them—got that way by reflecting constantly upon their troubles, those they had and those they expected to have. They are exponents of the art of anxiety.

One of the wisest men in the ancient Roman world was a Greek slave named Epictetus. He learned through practice the art of living without the inner turmoil caused by anxiety. He faced life with calm fortitude.

Epictetus had four possessions he could call his own. One of them was a lamp. A thief stole the lamp, but Epictetus did nothing about it.

"It is the thief who loses," he said. "I bought the lamp; it cost me a few pennies. But it cost the thief his soul."

In the *Discourses of Epictetus,* one of the prized books of inspiration on my study shelves, I found this, one of his characteristic sayings: "It does not make any difference what happens to you. Above all else, master the art of being calm." And Epictetus practiced what he preached.

A wise seventeenth-century Frenchman, by the name of La Rouchefoucauld, was credited with saying: "When a man finds no peace within himself, it is useless to look for it elsewhere."

Jesus was right when he insisted that peace is an inside job. The peace of God that passes all understanding must be generated from within, if it is to possess our lives without.

Help Yourself by Thinking of Others

A second thing that will help you face life without inner turmoil is to get self out of the center of focus. No self-centered life can hope to be blessed with inner quietness.

One of the surest ways to remove ourselves and our own anxieties from the center of our thinking is to reach out a helping hand to some fellow wayfarer. It is possible to lose one's life of anxiety, and find one's life in the deep satisfaction of helping some one worn out and depressed by the tensions of our day.

A woman was telling a friend about her sister. "My sister," she said, "suffers greatly from her belief. It makes her feet hurt."

"But," inquired her friend in astonishment, "how can her belief hurt her feet? What is her belief?"

"My sister," came the reply, "believes that she can wear a No. 2 shoe on a No. 6 foot."

I am thinking now of a woman who was always grumbling because her feet ached. Whether it was due to her trying to force a No. 6 foot into a No. 2 shoe I do not know. But she was silenced when she visited another woman with a radiant face and a loving heart, who could move neither hands nor feet, and who could not even turn her head without pain.

The way to stop thinking about ourselves is to think of others. If we cannot visit them, we can often write a cheering letter. We can always pray for them. And that may be the highest form of service one person can do for another.

I have known sufferers actually to be healed of their

own disabilities when they have sincerely prayed for someone else.

Recently I learned of a doctor who started a prayer circle among his patients. Writing about his experience he said: "I noticed that when a woman with a headache, giddiness and a dry throat, is asked to pray for a man afflicted with cancer, she at once feels better herself. She realizes that she might have worse diseases and starts to think about someone else's troubles rather than her own."

Thomas Carlyle said of the Book of Job: "There is nothing written, I think, in the Bible or out of it, of equal literary merit."

When one reads that ancient masterpiece he will find that Job was certainly afflicted not only with sores on his body but anxieties of the mind. But he found deliverance through a healthy insight.

How significant is the sentence: "The Lord turned the captivity of Job when he prayed for his friends." Job ceased to be a captive, the slave of his own ailments, when he forgot himself in praying for others.

You will find escape from your own mental turmoils as you begin to think about others and to pray for them. It will not only bring healing and strength and courage to others, but to yourself, for faith and courage and hope increase by the sharing of them.

Religion as a Way of Life

This leads naturally to the third thing I would like to say: If we are to face life without inner turmoil and with a quiet mind, we must make our religion function.

Religiously speaking there are three kinds of people in the world. First, there are those who make no profession of religion, nor any attempt to live the religious life.

Second, there are those who profess religion but do not

practice it. It is in this group that a great many church members belong. They have never really got any good from their religion.

Their religion promises them great things—such as power, joy, confidence, liberty, and contentment, and greatest of all a challenge. But a great many people who have attended churches for years have none the less to confess that they have never received these great blessings.

It is not only that they find they no longer believe many things that their fathers believed. That we all find. But they also feel that the great experiences of which others speak so joyfully have never come to them.

For religion is primarily an experience, and many have sought it, but not found it, asked for it, but not received it, knocked but never found before them an open door that leads to peace and joy and assurance that life is good. As I have said, many church members belong to this second group.

But there is a third group who not only profess their religion but practice it. These are the ones whose religion is more than a mere verbal expression of faith. Their religion is a way of life.

Running through it is a profound conviction that God is very near, that He is an available friend. They say every day, if not in exact words, nevertheless in spirit: "Into Thy hands I commit my spirit."

What a difference it would make in your life and mine if each morning we would make an offering of the day to God. Our anxieties would sink into "airy nothingness," if we started each day determined that we shall seek to know and to follow God's guidance during the next twenty-four hours.

We need the assurance that there is a purpose running through our lives, and that it is as irresistible as the flowing tides. Such an assurance would cause us to lose our self-importance as we yield ourselves to that purpose.

What a difference it would make in our lives just to know that whatever happens to us we are still in God's hands. If tragedy comes He is my strength and shield. If success should come my way, He is there to save me from the corrosion of pride, and to guide me and use me and my success for His glory and in the service of my fellow men.

To be rejected by God would be the only calamity that could ever happen to one. But we know that this would never happen, because God is love. His greatest promise to us is, "I will never leave you nor forsake you."

There may be times when we are terribly frightened, but we shall find peace, if we can feel ourselves always within the purposes of God. Isaiah tells us: "Thou wilt keep him in perfect peace whose mind is stayed on Thee."

The name of Hugh Redwood is an honored name in two fields in England—journalism and religion. He retired a few years ago. His vocation was journalism and his avocation was religion.

Once he told of a time in his life when he faced a grave crisis and the way in which he received help.[2] At this particular time he was under severe nervous strain. He did not know which course to take in the matter at hand.

He said he was staying at a friend's house a few hours before he was to speak at a public meeting. Several other people were present in the living room, engaging in conversation and laughing together. His host came over to him and asked Redwood if he would like to escape from the group and go upstairs for a brief rest. He replied that he would like it very much.

[2] Related by Leslie Weatherhead in *Prescription for Anxiety* (New York and Nashville: Abingdon Press, 1956), p. 113.

He was delighted to find a bright fire in the fireplace in the upstairs room, and beside an easy chair there was a little table with an open Bible upon it. He discovered that the Bible was open at Psalm 59, and he noted that someone had written in the margin an interpretation beside verse 10. In the King James Version of the Bible that verse reads as follows: "The God of my mercy shall prevent me." Of course the word "prevent" as used here has long since become obsolete. But as the ancient psalmist used it, it meant "go before." The interpretation written in the margin by an unknown hand was, "My God in His loving-kindness shall meet me at every corner."

Hugh Redwood said that it was like having a dark place illumined by the shining of a lamp. It was like a light from the very heart of God. Being greatly encouraged by the verse, he said that he made his decision and successfully turned a critical corner in his life. He went out from that experience, he said, expecting to find God at every crucial corner he had to turn in life.

Do you want to be able to face life without inner turmoil? Then begin practicing a new attitude of mind, learning to master the art of taking things as they come, not with indifference, but without anxiety. Change your focus of attention from self to helping others.

Make your religion something more than a Sunday affair, or a creed to be recited—make it function for you! Go out to meet each day saying with assurance: "My God in His loving-kindness shall meet me at every corner"—this day, and every day. And believe that He will!

Then you will have that most blessed of all things—a quiet mind in an unquiet world!

CHAPTER TEN

FINDING STRENGTH IN OUR WEAKNESS

When we consider the ability and the influence of the Apostle Paul he stands out as one of the greatest personalities in all human history. He carried the Christian religion from Asia over to the continent of Europe, and from there it came to us.

Paul wrote perhaps the most valuable letters that were ever written. In fact, they are the earliest Christian writings of which we have any knowledge, having appeared before the four Gospels were written. Thirteen of the twenty-seven books of the New Testament are letters written by Paul. No other man in history has done as much as he to formulate Christian thought.

The apostle was a bold adventurer, a daring pioneer. He was capable of standing up under all kinds of punishment without quitting. He suffered imprisonment, the scourging with whips, shipwreck, stoning, hunger, and threats to his life. These things were all a part of his daily experience.

Being the kind of man that he showed himself to be, it is almost startling to hear him confess that he had a weakness. In a letter to his friends in Corinth, he wrote: *"I was with you in weakness and in much fear and trembling."*

We are not to believe that Paul was just underrating himself, or that he was assuming a false sense of modesty.

He was sincere. There can be no doubt about it, for he was too much of a man to be insincere.

When he came near the end of his life and looked back upon his experiences, he did not hesitate to say: "I have fought a good fight, I have kept the faith." But in spite of his courageous, life-long fight against great odds, he confesses that he was no stranger to weakness and fear.

Most of those who have helped the world along would say the same. When one thinks of flowers and plants, he thinks of Luther Burbank. But in my reading recently, I was reminded that if it had not been for a physical weakness, we never would have heard of Burbank.

As a young man he was a semi-invalid. Worse still, he was filled with the fear that because of his illness he would be a failure in life. Finally, he changed his employment. He had been working in a hot, dusty factory in Worcester, Massachusetts. He quit that job and went to work in a plant nursery.

But those long New England winters further weakened his sick body. He then moved to California. He worked with plants outdoors in the warm climate, and became one of the world's greatest naturalists. It was Luther Burbank who said: "Every weed can be made a flower."

Had it not been for his sickness he would have spent his days in a hot dusty factory. Sometimes a weakness can be a blessing in disguise.

Demosthenes became the greatest orator of the ancient world, not in spite of a speech impediment, but because of a speech impediment. The weakness forced him to work more earnestly to perfect his speech. He put pebbles in his mouth and practiced speaking against the sound of the breakers on the beach. He failed time and again in his public appearances—but one day he stood before the people of Athens, the most perfect orator in the history of mankind. Out of his weakness came his strength.

(98)

Finding Strength in Our Weakness

Surely this should bring us comfort. When we are depressed by a failure, it rallies us to know that the experience is not confined to us. It is shared by all who have striven for an ideal.

The attainment of strength is nearly always the result of conquering weakness. No one was ever born a saint. Someone asked the question: "Why were the saints saints?" And he received the answer: "Because they were cheerful when it was hard to be cheerful, patient when it was hard to be patient, because they pushed on when they wanted to stay still, kept quiet when they wanted to talk, were agreeable when they felt like being disagreeable."

Those we most admire for the strength and consistency of their character have won it through weakness and fear.

But some of us feel our weakness so keenly that we allow it to paralyze us instead of impelling us to overcome it. We touch on some personal defect and quickly dismiss it saying: "But, then, that's my weakness. I guess I was born with it. Anyway I don't think there is anything to be done about it."

Whenever I am tempted to say that, or hear someone else say it, I am reminded of something the great John R. Mott once said: "You can become strongest in your weakest place."

How can we so manage our lives that we may find strength in our weakness?

Take a Positive Attitude Toward Weakness

First of all, you must learn to take a positive attitude toward your weakness.

When he was thrown into prison Paul wrote to his friends in Philippi: "I want you to know that what has happened to me has really served to advance the gospel."

Being thrown into prison enabled him to deliver his message to his guards, and through them reach their superiors in Caesar's household. That was taking a positive attitude toward his handicap.

A man who had known the ravages of illness, visited a friend of his in the hospital. Instead of sympathizing with him and leaving him steeped in self-pity, he challenged the bedridden man.

"I know you dislike being ill," he said to him, "and so did I when I was ill. But I find the only thing to do is to get something out of every experience that comes to me, good or bad. So make your illness give you something."

I am thinking now of a woman who did just that. The person who has discovered and revealed to the people of Arkansas their wild flowers is a shut-in, a woman crippled with arthritis. Although her hands are gnarled and twisted, she has painted exquisitely five hundred specimens of flowers. Harvard University wanted to buy the collection, but a public movement was launched to buy them for the state of Arkansas.

We are indebted to E. Stanley Jones for telling her story. When he visited her, he said that "Miss Whitfield cheerfully held up her twisted fingers and told how, by the law of compensation she was able to paint those delicate lines. Her cheer and her skill are beyond words. A shut-in knows more about the wild flowers and where they grow than anybody in the state!"

Accept Yourself

The editors of one of our magazines asks each week some prominent person to name the books that have most influenced his or her life. If you were asked that question, what books would you name?

I could name several, but one of the books that greatly

impressed me, so much so that I read it more than once, was that soul-stirring book by Perry Burgess, entitled *Who Walk Alone*.[1] It is the story of a young man who made triumph out of a disaster.

This young man had begun a happy and successful life, had arrived at a place of real standing in the community, and had become engaged to one of the most attractive girls in his home town. Then, suddenly he found himself one day looking at a door that had slammed shut in his face, shutting him off from all his future plans. He discovered that he was a leper.

And the way in which he faced that disaster, and yet managed to wring from it, in a positive way, a rich, useful, undaunted life, is one of the most dramatic, heartwarming stories one can read.

Just before going into a life-long exile on a distant Pacific island, his wise doctor friend spoke to him words of profound wisdom that the young man never forgot. The doctor said to him:

"You can take it standing up fighting, or you can lie down and let it beat you. And you're the only one who can say about that."

Perhaps the doctor little dreamed or realized that he was saying a great thing. And yet, here in a few words is one of the elementary and determining facts in human experience, namely, that whether the sound of a door slamming shut in your face is a death knell to your spirit, or a triumphant overture, depends upon whether you take a positive or a negative attitude toward it.

[1] New York: Henry Holt & Co., 1943.

Stop Comparing

In the second place, if you are to find strength in your weakness, you must stop comparing your lot in life with that of others.

Theodosia Garrison has a little poem in which she describes three entirely different people, all three of whom are facing the same inner problem. She pictures a housewife sitting by the open window of her little home, in early America, and working at her spinning wheel. Looking out of the window she sees two gypsies passing by on the road.

> The gypsies passed her little gate,
> She stopped her wheel to see:
> A brown-faced pair who walked the road
> Free as the wind is free.
> And suddenly her tidy room a prison seemed to be.
>
> Her shining plates against the walls,
> Her sunlit, sanded floor,
> The brass-bound wedding chest that held
> Her linen's snowy store,
> The very wheel whose humming died,
> Seemed only chains she bore.
>
> She watched the foot-free gypsies pass,
> She never knew or guessed
> The wistful dream that held them close,
> The longing in each breast:
> Some day to know a home like hers
> Wherein their hearts might rest.[2]

[2] "Dreamers" in Theodosia Garrison, *The Dreamers, and other Poems* (George H. Doran Co., 1917).

Finding Strength in Our Weakness

Here in this poem is a word picture of a human problem as old as history, and as universal as human life. The housewife longed to be a gypsy, and the gypsies longed to have a settled home like hers. The problem they faced was that of being willing to accept themselves and their lot in life without envying another.

And that is a problem that each of us faces, for even the best and bravest of us have days when we want to be anything but what we are. Many make themselves miserable by habitually measuring themselves by the achievements of other people.

They assume that they are responsible for not being as fortunate, useful, or happy as others are. We look upon our weakness and say: "Now if I was just as strong and unlimited as Mr. So and So."

Dr. Harry Emerson Fosdick in commenting upon this attitude has said: "It is a great day in a handicapped man's life when he makes up his mind that he has only one responsibility, not to be like anybody else, but to handle his special situation as well as he can."

Who can ever estimate the number of personal tragedies in this world caused by people being unwilling to accept themselves. You are forever going to be out of tune with life until you stop feeling responsible for being as fortunate or successful or happy or useful as some other person you know.

It was because he never gave way to envy or bitterness because his lot in life was not comparable to that of some other, but always accepted what life gave him and turned it to positive uses, that Paul was able to say within the walls of a prison: "I am ready for anything through the strength of the One Who lives within me."

The Place of God's Power

That last statement of Paul's leads us to say a third thing about finding strength in weakness: Your weakness can become the place where God's power is demonstrated.

Paul tells the Corinthians that he had come among them in weakness, in much fear and trembling. In a later letter he tells them of his experience with what he calls "a thorn in the flesh." We do not know its nature, though many ingenious conjectures have been made. Some have guessed it was epilepsy, a frequent accompaniment of genius.

Whatever it was, it hurt his pride, interfered with his work, gave him this sense of weakness and inferiority of which we have been thinking. "Three times," he said, "I sought the Lord that it should leave me, but He said to me: 'My grace is sufficient for you, for my power is made perfect in weakness.' Most gladly, therefore, will I glory in my weakness, for when I am weak, then I am strong."

The point of Paul's weakness could become the place of God's power. It could become a center through which that power could most fully radiate. Emerson in his essay on "Compensation" said: "No man had ever a defect that was not somewhere made useful to him."

History affords many illustrations of this truth. How many there have been who have done outstanding service for the human race who had to contend with a sense of their own deficiencies.

Moses had a stammering tongue. Standing one day before a burning bush, he heard God's call to become the deliverer of his nation. Like each one of us who is conscious of his weakness in the face of a great challenge, Moses began to protest, declaring that he was unfit for such a task. He thought of that speech defect of his.

"Who am I, that I should go to Pharaoh and bring the Children of Israel out of Egypt?" he protested. "I am not eloquent, for I am slow of speech, and just as slow in expressing my ideas." But God said to him: "What is that in your hand?"

"O this?" Moses said, holding up the shepherd's crook. "This is just a shepherd's rod, the simple badge of my occupation—all shepherds carry them."

"Throw it upon the ground before me," came the voice of the Eternal.

Moses obeyed the command. And lo! the simple shepherd's crook took on life and became a wriggling serpent. The shepherd was frightened and started to run from it, when the Voice said again: "Reach out your hand and take it by the tail."

Moses, trembling from head to foot, reluctantly did as he was bidden and the serpent became once more a rod in his hand. "You shall take this rod in your hand, and with it you shall become powerful," God said to him.

Moses, strengthened in his weakness, took the shepherd's rod with him as he turned his face toward Egypt, and in his hand it became a scepter of power, and he became a spiritual pioneer whose great moral precepts were to lay the foundations of civilizations unborn and undreamed.

Many a person through faith in God and the surrender of a weakness to Him has found the defect transformed into a stimulus.

Suppose your life does have a limited horizon. There's power in the Christian faith whereby such limitations can be accepted and used for great purposes.

Christianity is not an escape from reality. It does its greatest work for those who are broken by life, handicapped by weaknesses, or hindered by circumstances beyond their control.

Archibald Rutledge tells of an aged Negro man who had been hired as engineer on a small tugboat which ferried people across a Southern river. After he took over the job, the boat was transformed. The engine gleamed and shone, the floors were clean, the whole atmosphere was suggestive of order.

Mr. Rutledge sought out the engineer to congratulate him. He found him seated in the door of the engine room with an open Bible on his knee.

Mr. Rutledge asked him how he managed to bring about such a change in the appearance of the boat. "Cap'n," the old Negro man answered, "it's just this way: I'se got a glory!"

People limited by some weakness, people with mental and physical handicaps, have discovered the secret of triumphant living when they have allowed the glory of the Christian faith to lay hold of their weakness.

Christianity is not a creed—not an ecclesiastical system. Christianity is power! It gives radiance to the lives of those who practice it. It transforms people whose lot has been made difficult by some hardship, until they become towers of strength.

The Christian faith has the answer to your weakness, whatever it may be. It cannot always remove the weakness, but it can give you power to make something glorious out of it.

It is difficult for us to understand how God comes into our lives most readily, not where we are strong or successful, but where we are weak and where we fail. Sometimes it is only as we face an extreme situation in life that we acknowledge our need of Him. Our extremity becomes His opportunity.

One of the strange paradoxes of the Christian experience is, in the words of the Apostle Paul, that "when I am weak, then am I strong." It is then God says to us, as the Apostle says He said to him: "My grace is sufficient for you, for my power is made perfect in weakness."

And no matter who you are or what your past experiences have been, you will find this to be true!

CHAPTER ELEVEN

DON'T LET LIFE THROW YOU OFF BALANCE

Most of the advice we are given when we are young "goes in one ear and out the other." But occasionally some word of caution, some friendly admonition from an older person, for whom we have great respect, strikes home and is remembered far into adulthood. Sometimes in later years we may forget who said it, but not what he said.

Somewhere in my past, one of my elders—it may have been one of my parents, the minister of the local church, a schoolteacher, or perhaps a commencement speaker—spoke these words which still linger in my memory: "If you aspire to be a success in life, you must be prepared to meet with failure many times before you reach your goal. But whatever happens, don't let life throw you off balance."

Thomas á Kempis in *The Imitation of Christ* said the same thing in a different way. In pointing out the things which make for one's spiritual progress in this world, he said: "Whether things go well with you or otherwise, you go on thanking God in just the same way, letting nothing, good or bad, upset the even balance of your heart."

Thomas á Kempis seems to indicate, and rightly so, that it is possible to be thrown off balance by either good or bad, victory or defeat. For there is such a thing as victories that prove to be empty, and defeats that turn out to be victories. Rudyard Kipling in one of his poems reminds us that both success and failure can be impostors at times and must be treated just the same, else one may find himself thrown off balance by either of them.

Life never throws one off balance who has learned this truth that both victory and defeat can at times be impostors. So often they are not real, but pretenders to reality. Each has a way of parading in the disguise of the other. Victory sometimes comes dressed in sheep's clothing, and defeat is sometimes a sheep in wolf's clothing. And because no one handles life without coming to terms with this truth, it is well for us to examine it more closely.

Victory Can Be Defeat

For one thing, how often we are thrown off balance by thinking we have won a victory, only to find that victory is a defeat.

I am thinking now of a true story concerning a boy who got into a fight with his playmate. He overpowered his enemy, got him down in the gutter and sat upon him. As long as he held him down, he felt secure. But he was afraid to let him up for fear he might not be able to whip him a second time, if the fight were renewed.

After awhile he began to realize that he could keep the other boy down only so long as he stayed down in the gutter with him. But he wanted to get up and go on his way. He wanted to play with the other boys. Finally, he wanted to go home for dinner.

So he made terms with his enemy and let him up. His victory was an empty affair because it was the victim who named the terms.

It's a hard lesson for the world to learn that he who enslaves another is tied to his slave. The nation that enslaves another nation is not free; it is enslaved by its slave.

It appears that the conquering nation is truly the master

of the situation, but it is not. The conquering nation always lives in fear that its slave may somehow get the strength to strike back.

The Roman Empire became weak in its might. It enslaved too many people, who in turn held their master in subjection through fear that the slaves might rebel and throw off their shackles.

Spain was once a mighty nation, but she allowed her hunger for gold to spread her empire too thin. She became the slave of the people she enslaved. She was not free to use the gold she acquired as she wished, she had to spend most of it to keep in subjection the peoples from whom she took the gold.

What a tragic picture France presented to the world during World War II. She had boasted that she was on the winning side in World War I. But as a matter of history, France was enslaved by Germany for over two decades following the close of World War I.

In her struggle to keep Germany down, she was compelled to stay down with her. All of France's diplomacy, her economic policy, her press, were occupied during that time with the task of building and maintaining alliances against Germany, maintaining hostility to her, and preventing her recovery.

France had no freedom to develop her own preferred policies, to attend to her own national welfare, or to develop her own national genius. Her victory turned out to be an impostor, the conqueror was enslaved by the conquered, the victim becoming the victor.

How true it is in our personal living that we are so often defeated by our victories, that we fail in our successes.

In one of his poems, Alfred Noyes pictures a man materially successful in life, who suddenly realizes that he is a failure as far as life's satisfactions are concerned. As the

man comes to the end of his life, the ghosts of all his yes-
terdays rise up to haunt him, saying to him:

And after all the labor and the pains,
After the heaping up of gold on gold,
After success that locked your feet in chains
Had left you with a heart so tired and old:

Strange, is it not? To find your chief desire
Is what you might have had for nothing then—
The face of love beside a cottage fire
And friendly laughter with your fellow-men?

You were so rich when fools esteemed you poor.
You ruled a field that kings could never buy,
The glory of the sea was at your door,
And all those quiet stars were in your sky.

The nook of ferns below the breathless wood
Where one lone book could unlock Paradise—
What will you give us now for that lost good?
Better forget. You cannot pay the price.

You left them for the fame in which you trust.
But youth and hope—did you forsake them too?
Courage! When dust at length returns to dust
In your last dreams they may come back to you.[1]

Here was a man whose material victory was an impostor—it was defeat in disguise.

Defeat Can Be Victory in Disguise

But let us look at the other side of the picture. Not only
is victory sometimes empty—defeat in disguise—but how

[1] "To A Successful Man" in Alfred Noyes, *Collected Poems* (Philadel-
phia: J. B. Lippincott Company).

often defeat turns out to be an impostor—victory in disguise.

How often we are thrown off balance by thinking we have been defeated, only to find that defeat is a victory. The supreme successes of the world have been what the world calls defeats.

How we need that message in America—we who think of success only in terms of outward things: money, winning scores, or majority votes. We Americans say:

"Of course you can win in life! Just blow on your hands, have faith in yourself, and nothing is impossible."

But sometimes we can't win outwardly. Sometimes we have to face defeat externally. There are times when things go to pieces around our lives, and become as hopeless as Humpty Dumpty after he took his great fall.

But there is another word that is true: Even in defeat one can win the kind of victory that has meant most to the world.

We can afford to fail, if by our sacrifice the cause or principle for which we stand holds its ground.

In that great play of Channing Pollock's, *The House Beautiful,* the hero on his deathbed says to his wife: "I've been a failure, Jen. I've wound up right where I started."

But his wife replied as she soothes his fevered brow: "It's a great thing to wind up where you started, if you're holding a fort, your home, or your own soul."

For, she might have added, to do so is to win out in life, when to all appearances you have lost.

I remember a great football player who lost a game for his team because he refused to cheat. In making what would have proved to be the winning score, he accidentally made an illegal play. No one was aware of it but himself.

And while the crowd was cheering him and his teammates were congratulating him, he made his way to the referee and said:

"That play must not be allowed, because I did an illegal thing." He then explained what he had done, and of course the play was not allowed.

His teammates condemned him for his actions—for, after all, they argued, the referee hadn't seen it. And the team's supporters in the stands turned their cheers into jeers when they learned what had happened. His action cost his team the game.

But after a few days of reflection, his teammates came around and apologized for what they had said to him. And he soon became the hero of the campus. His teammates, the students, and finally the loyal supporters of the team came to see that the school had not really lost that day—they had won a great victory, greater than if the winning score had been in their favor.

It was a victory that brought the school the reputation of being a place where honor and sportsmanship were considered more important than championships. It became known as the school that was "too proud to cheat." It was victory rising phoenix-like from the ashes of defeat. Their defeat turned out to be an impostor.

One of the most inspiring little books that has come into my hands is one by Miss Helen Keller entitled: *Let Us Have Faith*.[2] Its inspiration results not so much from what she writes, but from the fact that Miss Keller, in spite of her physical handicaps, writes about faith.

As a child Miss Keller faced the possibility of living a defeated life because of her limitations of sight, hearing and speech. But with the help of Annie Sullivan, her devoted teacher, she showed up misfortune for what it was—

[2] Doubleday & Company, Inc., 1940

—an impostor—and she rose up to win one of the shining victories of human history.

That is a most indispensable kind of victory. Mankind can get along without material triumphs, we can get along without more efficient plumbing, better automobiles, or faster jet planes, or without even putting a man on the moon. But mankind cannot muddle on without this kind of inner victory—triumph on a cross, success in defeat.

There is not a person who needs to be a failure. No matter what happens on the outside, you need not fail within. Outwardly you may be defeated, you may go to your grave without achieving a victory in that realm. In fact, it's much easier to succeed outwardly than to succeed inwardly.

But the spiritual enrichment of mankind has come chiefly not from the men and women who succeeded outwardly, but from the men and women, who, though defeated, won an inner triumph of character.

Socrates, outwardly defeated, went to his death, inwardly victorious. Jesus of Nazareth nailed to a cross, the symbol of defeat in his day, so accepted it that ever since, when we think of a symbol of victory, we hold up the cross and say: "By this sign conquer!"

Each of us thinks of someone we have known and loved —to whom life was not kind—but who within the limits of defeat won a success that has been the major inspiration of our lives.

The Secret of St. Paul

It cannot be said too often that God holds us responsible, neither for our defeats or our victories, but for the way we stand up to life.

It has always seemed to me—and I say it reverently—

that there is a Divine Sportsmanship about God. He places us in a world where we are subjected to either defeat or victory, but He makes available to us the power to triumph, whatever the turn of affairs. Life will never throw you off balance if you can meet with triumph and disaster, and treat those two impostors just the same.

And you can, for the Apostle Paul did, and he tells us how he managed to do it. He says (using the New English Translation): "I have learned to find resources in myself whatever the circumstances. I know what it is to be brought low, and I know what it is to have plenty. I have been thoroughly initiated into the human lot with its ups and downs—fullness and hunger—plenty and want."

Paul knew both success and failure, and took them in stride, without being thrown off balance. But we want to know more—we know that he had the resources in himself to handle whatever came to him in life. But how did he get that way? This is what we need to know.

And so we step up to his prison bars and ask him a pointed question: "Tell us, Paul, what is your secret?" And with the light of faith in his eyes, and the strength of courage in his voice, he replies (using once more the New English Translation): "I have strength for anything through Him who gives me power."

That's the secret of Paul's victorious life. That is the secret of all the brave ones of earth who "meet with triumph and disaster and treat those two impostors just the same," and are thereby not thrown off balance by anything that may happen to them.

"Tell Us How to Die"

Among the moving stories which come out of World War I was an incident in connection with a variety entertainment that was given for some of the men in London

just before they left for the front-line trenches. At the close
of the entertainment, a young officer arose, at his colonel's
request, to express to the entertainers the men's thanks.
This he did in genial words of charm and good humor.

Then suddenly, as if in afterthought, and in a serious
mood, he said:

"We men are soon crossing to France, and to the
trenches, and, very possibly, of course, to death. Will any
of you, who have so graciously entertained us, tell us how
to die?"

That was a big order, and one, I dare say, you and I
would choose not to have asked of us. As was expected, the
question fell on the group of entertainers like a bombshell.
There was a strained silence for a few minutes, no one apparently knowing just what to say.

Then the answer came from an unexpected source, and
in an unexpected manner. One of the women singers who
a few minutes before had entertained the men with a
number of rollicking songs, made her way quietly to the
front of the stage. Without musical accompaniment, she
began to sing that great aria from *Elijah*.

"O rest in the Lord, wait patiently for Him,
And He shall give thee thy heart's desire.
Commit thy ways unto Him, and trust in Him."

That young entertainer had the right answer. For is not
that the answer to each of our needs, if we are to be adequate—not for death alone, but for life? Each of us needs
a heart and mind that has come to rest in the Eternal God,
for, as St. Augustine has said: "O God, our hearts are restless, until they find rest in Thee."

When your heart comes to rest in God and all your ways
are committed to His will, then you will let nothing, good
or bad, upset the even balance of your heart.

CHAPTER TWELVE

LIFE HAS ITS BRIGHT SPOTS

There's a line in the Book of Job which could be used as a poetic description of all those who take a gloomy, pessimistic, humorless view of life. It reads: "Men see not the bright light which is in the clouds."

It is especially descriptive of those who are lacking a sense of humor. There are those who are either unable or unwilling to see the bright spots in life.

This is an appropriate time to talk about having a sense of humor, for so many people are losing, or have already lost their lightheartedness, because of the chaotic condition of our world. Even those whose general disposition is inclined to be cheerful, have difficulty these days seeing a bright light in the clouds which overshadow our world.

Certainly a sense of humor should have a place among those indispensable qualities of mind and spirit which enable us to face life without losing heart. It is a great tension reliever and a lot less expensive than tranquilizers.

All of us are inclined in days like these to become overly tense, and this tenseness is exacting a heavy toll. You and I were not made to live constantly under stress and strain without some relief. Sooner or later "something's got to give"—in the body or in the mind.

A sense of humor, the ability to see the bright spots that are in an otherwise serious situation, keeps one from taking life or himself too seriously. There is much truth in the saying that God gave us humor to keep us from going mad.

A typical English weather bureau report runs something like this: "Rain, thundershowers, fog, mist, disagreeable weather, with bright intervals." There are bright intervals in life as in weather, but it usually takes one with a sense of humor to recognize them.

The Five Allies of Faith

During the fall and winter of 1940 the city of London went through the fiery furnace of affliction. Night after night the city trembled with the vibration caused by the firing of guns, the explosion of bombs, and the falling of buildings.

At dusk the siren, warning the city of imminent danger would wail its melancholy message, and the "all clear" signal would bring its welcome relief just before six o'clock in the morning. All through the long hideous night the din went on.

Night after night that was the history of London in those days. In one month 7000 were killed and 10,000 injured. Thousands were made homeless. Each evening multitudes bought tickets for the Underground and, admitted to the platform, stayed there all night.

The only light to be seen in the clouds in those days was caused by the explosion of Nazi bombs, and the bursting of shells from the ground defenses.

In such a time of agony, sorrow, and suffering the task of the minister of religion was a difficult one. Amid the darkness and despair people needed God as never before.

One of London's distinguished ministers during that period, who is still recognized as one of the world's best-known religious leaders, was Leslie Weatherhead. His church, the City Temple, the center of Protestantism in the city, was destroyed by Nazi bombs. He and his congregation met whenever they could in a borrowed church sanctuary.

In the midst of those tragic days Leslie Weatherhead wrote a book. The title was, *This Is the Victory.*[1] It was a collection of the sermons and addresses he had delivered to his distraught congregation.

In the first section of the book were eight of his messages describing the nature of the Christian faith. A second section set forth five of the allies of faith, and a third section contained three messages of faith and the future.

It is the second section of the book which intrigued me. What are the allies of faith? Weatherhead lists beauty, patience, hope, truth and, of all things, he names humor.

The Value of a Laugh

In normal times one would not be startled to find humor listed as an ally of faith, but to hear a message on humor as an ally of faith in the midst of tragedy, well, that was startling!

Knowing the background against which the book is written, one is inclined to say, as Dr. Weatherhead suspects many did say: "Here is the world falling to pieces about our heads, and he devotes a chapter to an unimportant trifle like humor!"

But Dr. Weatherhead defends himself by saying that it is in just such a time when people's nerves are on edge that humor is needed to give a lift to one's faith.

It is really a great gift to be able to see the bright side of things—to be able to see "the bright light which is in the clouds." If such a gift of humor is needed in the midst of the crises and tragedies of life, certainly it is needed in less strenuous times as well.

[1] New York and Nashville: Abingdon-Cokesbury Press, 1941.

It is one of the best solvents in the world for the "grit of irritation that gets into the cogs of life." And the person who can laugh at himself, as well as with others, will be among the last casualties in the war of nerves waged by life.

Humor has probably done more to maintain the mental balance of persons under strain than any other factor, except prayer. The business of living is much too serious to be taken solemnly—taken responsibly, yes, but with pompous solemnity, never! When the tensions of life are tight, and we are all tied up in knots, a hearty laugh lightens the strain.

Humor and Your Health

Attention has been called to the fact that in cases of insanity, humor is utterly lacking. Humor makes for sanity and health. It allays hostility and oils the machinery of human relationships.

One of the first requirements for a man who is to become and remain a totalitarian dictator is that he be totally lacking in a sense of humor. Men like the late, but not lamented, Mussolini, Hitler, and Stalin, and like the present day dictators—Franco, Castro, and Khrushchev—dare not have a sense of humor and expect to hold their places of despotic power. For to have a sense of humor means that you must know how to laugh at yourself—and enjoy others' laughter at your expense—and this a dictator could never do.

On the other hand, you can hardly think of a stalwart, dynamic personality whom men love to remember for his lasting contribution to the human race, who was not blessed with a sense of humor.

Abraham Lincoln at once comes to mind. His humor

was typically American. Yet, no man in our history ever carried a greater burden of sorrow than did he.

When the burden of the nation's anguish rested upon his soul, he said: "If what I feel were equally distributed to the whole of the human family, there would not be one cheerful person in all the earth."

During the most trying days of the Civil War, he once remarked to a gloomy set of surrounding officials: "Gentlemen, why don't you laugh? With the fearful strain I should die without laughter."

Two Quaker ladies were discussing the prospective outcome of the Civil War. One said that she thought Jefferson Davis would win because he was a praying man. The other lady said that Abraham Lincoln was also a praying man. The first replied: "Yes, but he is so given to jokes that the Lord will not know whether or not he is in earnest when he prays."

There Is a Time to Laugh

"But," someone asks, "what has all this got to do with religion?"

It has plenty to do with it. I agree with Dr. Weatherhead that a sense of humor is an ally of faith, because it is of God. It is one of the faculties God has planted within us to save us from taking ourselves too seriously, becoming pompous and conceited, or even going mad.

It helps keep religion wholesome and balanced. Your laughing has a place as well as your praying. There's a "time to weep and a time to laugh," says the writer of Ecclesiastes.

Fanatics in religion are usually devoid of humor. They say with solemnity that laughter has no place in true religion.

Even our forefathers did not think that faith and fun

ever mixed. They seemed to think that if a thing was enjoyable, it mattered not how decent, wholesome and clean it was, it was wrong. In the third edition of Cruden's "Concordance of the Bible" published in 1769, we read: "To laugh is to be merry in a sinful manner."

When I was a small boy, living on a Tennessee farm, I heard many stories told concerning Sam Jones, an eccentric evangelist of the Southern Methodist Church, of which my parents were members. The stories he told himself and the stories told about him are legion.

No man with a heart so tender ever dealt in language so strong. When referring to the sinners, he made use of the rough terms, "scoundrel," "fool," "lying rascal," "red-nosed devil" and the like. On one occasion he said: "If any man don't like what I say, let him come up to me afterward and say so, and I'll forgive him."

But much of his wholesome philosophy is summed up in these words: "I'll tell you how I've stood all I've been through. I'm always in a good humor. I believe that fun is the next best thing to religion. And if religion can't triumph over temperament, it ain't much account."

Jesus Was a Man of Joy

I believe that Jesus was a man of humor. We have come to think of him as a man of sorrows and acquainted with grief. So he was, but I believe that he was also a man of radiant joy and acquainted with laughter.

In fact, most of those who have the keenest sense of humor have known the profoundest depths of sorrow and disappointment. It is my conviction that pain and joy have common roots in human life.

The record is that twice Jesus wept, and no mention is made of His laughter. The natural inference is that His laughter was not an exceptional occurrence. It may be that the reason the writers of the gospels mention the fact that Jesus wept, was that it was so unusual.

It is impossible for me to hold in my mind the thought of Jesus as a perfect man, if we exclude all humor from His personality.

The Master even got the reputation of being a frequent guest at gay parties, banquets, and weddings. I believe He could have gone to the stodgiest church party and made it blaze with fun and happiness. He would be the life and soul of any party. His enemies called Him "a gluttonous man and a wine drinker."

How could a man without humor be popular at parties, banquets, and weddings? How could such a man be the kind of a person to whom children would run? How could he be the kind of person of whom it was said "the common people heard Him gladly"?

I dare to believe that if we had met the Master along the roads of Galilee and Judea during His lifetime—and centuries before the pompous ecclesiastics took over the organization of his mission into a church, and the stodgy theologians took over the interpretation of Him and His teachings—we would have been impressed by His gaiety, His healthy laughter, and the humor which bubbled up from His deep joy.

I am convinced that Jesus used humor in His illustrations. It is inconceivable that no ripple of laughter passed over the crowd, or that no humor was intended in His vivid picture of the fat old Pharisee drinking soup, straining out a gnat, and swallowing a camel.

Just shut your eyes and imagine the camel going down! Dr. T. R. Glover in his book *The Jesus of History* writes:

"How many of us have ever pictured the process, and the series of sensations, as the long, hairy neck slid down the throat of the Pharisee—all that amplitude of loose-hung anatomy—the hump, two humps—both of them slid

down, and he never noticed—and the legs—all of them—
with the whole outfit of knees and big-padded feet. The
Pharisee swallowed a camel and never noticed it."

But a gnat got in his soup, and he very carefully picked
it up, wrung it out, and threw it aside.

And then there is another man fumbling to remove a
piece of sawdust from his brother's eye, when a great
plank sticks out of his own.

So Jesus not only used humor, but exaggerated humor
at that.

Jesus was a man of sorrows and acquainted with grief?
Yes, He was, but He was a man with a deep joy.

We must remember that when all is said about joy, its
opposite is not sorrow. We speak of the "joys and sorrows
of life" as though they are opposites, but they are not
really such.

Sorrow and joy can be held in the mind at the same
time. Note what was said of Jesus: "Who for the joy that
was set before him endured the cross." He experienced
joy and endured sorrow at the same time.

Again and again in our experience, laughter and tears
are close relatives in our family of feelings. The opposite
of joy is not sorrow, but unbelief.

The New Testament contains much that is sorrowful,
but it begins with the songs of joy around the cradle of a
Child, and ends with the Hallelujah Chorus sung by all
the ransomed hosts of heaven.

The Christian Cheer

No one has more right to humor than the Christian. The
materialist, or the secularist, the man of the world, he
whose trust is in things, may become dismayed when his
world goes to pieces about him.

But the Christian knows that the worthwhile things

cannot perish. The Christian sees the suffering and sin and sorrow of the world, and his laughter may often be momentarily silenced, but his joy no man can take away from him.

In spite of the dark facts of life—its sin and sorrow and suffering—the Christian has listened to the Good News about life and the universe, and believes what he has heard, and goes through life rejoicing.

When life becomes dark and forbidding about us, and worst comes to worst, the Christian should be like the Cheshire cat in *Alice in Wonderland,* and let the grin be the last thing to vanish.

As long as there is humor, there is life, and where there is life there is hope. For to laugh means that the happenings around us have not got us down, and that our faith is still victorious.

The world is truly in a mess, and no one has to tell a Christian that. But the Christian hears a joyous Voice come ringing down the centuries from a Man standing in the very shadow of death, with the sorrows of the world in His heart, but with the laughter of heaven in His eyes. And He says to us: "Be of good cheer. I have overcome the world."

He knew how to see the bright light in the clouds that gathered about Him. And so can we, if we keep our faith in Him and in the God of joy and peace whom He taught us to love, and worship, and trust with our lives.

CHAPTER THIRTEEN

LEARNING TO OUTWIT YOUR YEARS

A few years ago I received through the mail a clipping from a Nashville, Tennessee, newspaper telling about a civil engineer who had retired and settled down in a small town in southern Kentucky. It said a lot of people in that little town will tell you that the luckiest break they ever had was when this man decided to retire and live there.

"Decided" is not the right word, for he was forced to retire because of his age, after twenty-six years as a maintenance engineer for the Florida Highway Department. At the time he was sixty-nine years of age, which was four years past the regular retirement age.

Now, according to the newspaper account, this retired civil engineer is probably busier than ever, and it's a good thing for that little Kentucky town that he is. They and many other communities could use a lot of retired men with his vigor and civic pride.

For three years he worked almost full-time driving a state-owned bookmobile through two counties, handing out books to eager youngsters. It was a library on wheels. He didn't particularly want that kind of a job, but he wanted to keep busy doing something useful.

"I took it because I was afraid no one else would," he said, "and it's vital that children have a chance to read. I wish there had been something like that when I was growing up. I went through the entire library in a few months at the little prep school I attended when I was a boy."

That little Kentucky town, where he came to live in retirement, now has a fine new city reservoir that might not be there if it hadn't been for him. Plagued by periodic water shortages, city officials decided a reservoir was the answer. But the budget couldn't afford the strain of a team of engineers. So the city fathers approached this retired engineer hesitatingly. But they shouldn't have worried. He quickly accepted because the reservoir was very important to the health and well-being of the community.

Coaching Little League at Eighty

Youngsters in the little town treat him with the adulation they reserve for genuine sports heroes. They know that he was an outstanding fullback on the football teams of a great university during the years of 1906 through 1908. They also know that he was a great baseball pitcher in his younger days. But all that happened before even their fathers and mothers were born.

They worship this man, who is now approaching his eightieth birthday, because he coaches a Little League baseball team each summer in addition to managing the town's water department. And he teaches the boys the proper approach to sports—winning isn't the most important thing to him. His team ended up in the league cellar a few years ago. "But the boys had a lot of fun," he says with a smile. One crippled youngster played on the team, and the boost it gave his morale was worth more than victories to their coach.

He had to pass an examination for a license before the state would accept him as the engineer on the reservoir project. He passed the examination with flying colors. Whatever the conversation may be he will manage to bring it around to his current job as engineer for the town's water system. He seems to get greater satisfaction out of that present position of his than the far greater engineering projects for which he has been responsible during his distinguished engineering career. "It keeps me busy," he says, "and I like to keep busy."

Here is a good example of a "senior citizen" who has made up his mind to keep alive as long as he lives. He has learned the secret of outwitting his years. The newspaper clipping I know to be true, because that retired engineer is Dwight Morrison of Elkton, Kentucky, an older brother of mine.

My brother's life since retirement would indicate that he has read and agrees with Robert Browning that the last of life is that for which the first was made. The English poet was convinced that in a life well-lived each succeeding day becomes better than the last; that each day, each year, each experience does not stand alone, that it cannot be separated from what has happened before or what may happen afterward. Browning further believed that in a life well-lived each period or stage brings its own distinctive riches and satisfactions.

I am thinking now of another man of eighty years who was asked the question: "What season of life is the happiest?" and he answered by pointing to a grove of trees in front of his house.

"When spring comes and in the soft air the buds are breaking on the trees," he said, "and they are crowned with blossoms, I think how beautiful is spring! But when summer comes and covers the trees with heavy foliage and singing birds are among the branches, I think how beautiful is summer! And then, when fall loads the trees with golden fruit and the leaves begin to bear those gorgeous tints, I cannot help thinking how beautiful is autumn!

"But winter comes, and there is neither foliage nor fruit. But I have only to look up, and there through the leafless branches I see what was hidden before—the stars of heaven shining through!"

If you learn to outwit your years and keep alive as long as you live with ever enriching experiences and interests, then each stage of your life will bring its own distinctive satisfactions. How is this to be done?

Keep the Wondering Mind

In the first place, one must never stop learning and growing mentally. One must keep the wondering mind.

There is a man living in a small city in the Midwest—or at least he was living the last I heard of him—who is seventy-seven years of age, and if anyone asks him how he is feeling, he has only one reply: "I'm seventy-seven years of age and I'm fading fast."

One day a friend met him crossing the street. Cars were whizzing by in both directions. "How are you feeling, Grandpa," his friend inquired. And he received the familiar reply: "I'm seventy-seven years of age and I'm fading fast."

His friend took him by the arm and said: "Come over to the curb and get out of the street and you may live to be seventy-eight!"

In contrast to that seventy-seven-year-old man, who is living but is not alive, is another seventy-seven-year-old man it was my privilege to know. When I was serving my first church in Dallas, Texas, I became intimately acquainted with a very fine Christian gentleman named Baxter P. Fullerton. He was the ad interim minister of the City Temple Presbyterian Church in that city until they could call a pastor.

During his seventy-seven years of life Dr. Fullerton had been a busy man, having rendered distinguished service for the church. He had been called out of retirement to take over the temporary responsibility at the City Temple.

One day I met him on the street just before he left on his summer vacation. I asked him how he was going to spend the four weeks away from his work.

"Well," he said, "I'm taking along a box of the latest books on religious education, and I plan to spend my vacation time reading them. You know, Max, we young fellows are going to have to keep abreast of the times and keep looking forward, if we ever expect to get anywhere."

There was the spirit of youthful alertness in a seventy-seven-year-old man. I wish it were possible somehow to telescope the years of my early ministry and these later years together and be able to introduce Dr. Fullerton, whom I knew in my early ministry, to a man whom it was my privilege to meet in these last few years of my ministry. He was the late Dr. Merle Smith, for twenty-five years the beloved minister of the First Methodist Church of Pasadena. Dr. Fullerton and Dr. Smith would have enjoyed each other, for they were of the same quality of mind and spirit.

Dr. Merle Smith was a man who kept his interest in life to the very last. He was always on the intellectual line of march, seeking to learn something new each day.

While confined to his home during the last years of his life, he was visited by me one day and I found him absorbed in a new book on travel. He was full of excitement as he described to me some of the thrilling things he had learned about a distant and little visited section of the world.

Whenever I talked to Dr. Smith it was like taking an intellectual and spiritual tonic. Although he died before the advent of that popular song, "Young at Heart," its words could have been written by someone who had just paid a visit to this wonderful Methodist minister: "It's hard, you will find, to be narrow of mind, if you are young

at heart . . . For life gets more exciting each passing day
. . . if you are among the very young at heart."[1]

Some people seem to think that all an older person needs
is "precious memories." There is not much pleasure in
spending your days counting your memories like beads
on a rosary. Cicero is not much help to one trying to adjust
to old age when he says: "The harvest of old age is the
recollection of blessings previously secured." That might
be a good way to spend a few minutes, but not a series of
years.

Stephen and Rosemary Benét end their poem on Lincoln with these words: "Lincoln was the green tree, Lincoln kept on growing."[2] That is the way it should be. The
men and women who daily improve mentally and spiritually will not bore their younger friends by beginning
too many sentences with "When I was young . . ."

Being alive to the present, with a hopeful eye to the
future, will help to overcome even hardening of arteries.
When you lose the spirit of meeting new circumstances
with some degree of zest, you are getting very old in mind.
That one knows how to take the years in stride who is con-
tinuously interested in worthy enterprises, and retains an
alertness of mind. For a person's age does not depend upon
his accumulated birthdays, but upon the elasticity of his
spirit, the vigor of his mind.

Beware of Self-pity

In the second place, if one is to outwit his years, he will
never waste energy in self-centeredness, it matters not how
rough life has been to him.

[1] By permission of copyright owner. Copyright 1954, Cherio Music Publishers, Inc.
[2] Stephen and Rosemary Benét, "Lincoln" in *A Book of Americans* (New
York: Holt, Rinehart & Winston, 1933).

Some months after the death of a member of her family, a woman came to see me. Life had come to a stop for her when her loved one died. She refused to be reconciled to the fact. She was overwhelmed with self-pity.

She said to me: "I am so unhappy I have reached the point where I do not care to see anyone or go any place. I read the Bible each day but I have not been to church since she left us."

I had great sympathy for that woman, as I have for anyone who is grieving over the loss of a loved one. But in fairness to her I felt the time had come for someone to do some straight talking to her. I foolishly elected myself to be the one to do it, even though I knew I ran the risk of losing her friendship. I felt compelled to say to her: "You had better be on your guard against indulging too much and too long in self-pity through your suffering and loss. You have a husband, children, good health, a home to manage and a mind and soul to cultivate. You will show your true self not as you withdraw from life but as you accept reality and respond to the claims life lays upon you. Remember: Life must go on, in spite of everything."

I told her that beyond a certain point she was indulging in weakness and perhaps unconsciously enjoying the attention she was receiving. It was a harsh thing to say to her, but I was persuaded that it was time she began to make the ascent out of the deep well of despondency and self-pity into which she had fallen. For she had forgotten the purpose of her being here, and needed to hear the blunt truth, as it was once stated by Disraeli, who knew something about the meaning of sorrow and suffering, that "grief is the agony of an instant; the indulgence of grief the blunder of a life."

Although her first reaction was one of resentment, she later thanked me for speaking frankly to her. She later accepted the fact of her loved one's death, and has begun to live a creative life.

How different was the way in which the great actress Helen Hayes accepted the great tragedy of her life! Perhaps you know of the loss she suffered in the death of her nineteen-year-old daughter Mary, just before the mother and daughter were to have appeared together in a Broadway play.

In writing about it in a magazine article, Miss Hayes said: "I have found comfort in doing, in visiting those who have been struck down, the children and the parents, in thinking that through Mary's death perhaps she and I were destined to have a little part in the final victory. I have learned ineffable gratitude for the Scriptural commandment to love thy neighbor as thyself. Now at last I know the solace that comes from its meaning. Once I thought it old-fashioned, empty, but it now shines with a new radiance out of the depths of its truth and simplicity."

If we are to outwit our years, command them and not be ruled by them, we must make it our goal to give the best that is within us, and not leave behind ugliness, self-pity, and anger toward life. That man knew how to meet life with the eyes of his soul turned outward rather than inward who wrote: "I shall pass through this world but once. If, therefore, there be any kindness I can show or any good thing I can do, let me do it now. Let me not defer it or neglect it, for I shall not pass this way again."

Life is much too brief for us to waste its energies in an all consuming attention to ourselves exclusively.

The Fourth of July Letter

But nothing keeps one alive and alert all his life like a vital first hand religious faith. Neither life nor death is intimidating to those who have the assurance that they do not walk alone, but that there walks with them across the years a Divine Companion.

Dr. Clarence William Lieb wrote a book some years ago entitled *Outwitting Your Years*.[3] This book is an outgrowth of his experience as a doctor specializing in diseases of older people. It is a good textbook for those who would keep alive—not only physically, but mentally and spiritually. After discussing all the things that contribute to a wholesome life, near the end of his book he expresses his own gratitude for what his religion has meant to him. He says that after everything else has been considered the supreme alchemy in the process of outwitting the years is belief in God.

Life never becomes dull to those who have a vital faith in God, because they have tapped a source of power which keeps life always new and fresh.

I am reminded of one of the most engaging and energetic persons one could ever know. He was an old teacher of mine when I was a prep school student. His favorite text of scripture was the closing verse of Psalm 23: "Surely goodness and mercy shall follow me all the days of my life, and I shall dwell in the house of the Lord forever."

In a mimeographed letter to all his former students following the death of his wife, he confessed that the two of them through their long married life had repeated together the Shepherd's Psalm each night before they went to bed.

When we were his students, he asked each one of us to write him a letter on the Fourth of July telling him our plans for the coming year. In the letter following his wife's death he wrote: *"You will recall that I annually requested at the close of school a card or letter on July 4th., telling*

3 New York: Prentice-Hall, Inc., 1949.

me of the next year's plans. This is my 'Fourth of July letter' to you. This next year and for many years in the future, we must carry on in helping, as best we can, to establish our Father's kingdom! God is good to us and we must keep heads up and hearts aglow!"

The words of the psalmist were real to that old professor of mine! And as a result, "goodness and mercy" did follow him all the days of his life—even "through the valley of the shadow of death"—and he was always conscious of the fact that he "dwelt in the house of the Lord forever."

To really keep alive as long as you live and achieve self-fulfillment is to bring God from the shadowy circumference of your life, where so many keep Him, into the very center of your life. When this is done, the vitality, the sense of wonder, and the boundless interest in life will never wane. Both the mind and heart will be renewed, not once, but day by day, and year by year.

CHAPTER FOURTEEN

FAITH TO FACE LIFE'S FINALE

John Erskine, an eminent Scottish theologian, once said: "He who fears death has missed the point of life." No one can achieve a well-rounded view of life who fails to come to terms with the fact of death. We all know that we are going to die some day; in fact, it is the only thing that we know of what is in store for us. All the rest is mere guess work and most of the time we guess wrong.

There are two extreme attitudes which people quite often adopt toward the end of this earthly life.

There are those who resolutely refuse to face the fact of death. An American psychologist advises: "Never allow yourself a passing thought of death." The late William Randolph Hearst was said to have prohibited anyone mentioning it in his presence.

To the other extreme are those who permit their minds to dwell too often upon thoughts of death. King Philip of Macedon employed a slave to break into his room each day and cry out: "Philip, remember thou must die."

Now both of these attitudes are, as I have said, extreme. It is unrealistic to go through life giving no thought to the inevitable finality of this life. But on the other hand, it is morbid and unhealthy to dwell upon it constantly.

More positive and wholesome is the attitude reflected in a comment made by the late General Jan Smuts of South Africa, when he said: "As we grow older, life comes to consist of memories—and the Great Hope."

Can we find a philosophy that will give us light at the end of life's road? Is there anything which can change our timid hope that death may not be the end into a certain confidence of life beyond the grave? In other words, can we discover a faith to face life's finale?

I believe that such a faith can be achieved. How is it to be done? Let me offer three suggestions.

Learn to Live First

In the first place, if you are to have a faith to face the inevitability of death, you must first have a zest for living.

A faith which lifts the burden of the fear of death, must be able to make life every day an experience in abundant living. Brooding thoughts of death have little room in the mind of one whose years are made rich by happy human relationships.

Montaigne had that in mind when he said: "He who would teach men to die must first teach them to live." When life is full and abundant with the joy of living, the love of one's fellow men, and abounding in good works, there is neither time nor place for anxiety concerning the life here or hereafter.

The late Oliver Wendell Holmes, associate justice of the United States Supreme Court, had that sort of zest for living. On his ninetieth birthday a group of his Harvard friends gave him a radio birthday party.

Justice Holmes concluded an impressive speech of response over a national radio network by quoting the words of a Latin poet:

> "Death plucks me by the ear and says,
> 'Live—I am coming.'"

His voice reflected on that occasion his consuming interest in life and the inner strength which he had always been able to muster for the task.

His biographer said of him: "The very act of waking each day had been exciting, with the battle waiting. 'Bugler, blow that charge. I am ready.'" Death could offer no problem to such a spirit. His enthusiasm for living made each hour a triumph, and made him eager for eternal life.

A group of women were discussing the unexpected passing of a dear friend, when one of the group tried to explain why death seemed so terrifying. "Death is so, well, it's so final," she said.

The end of life always seems final to those who have built their major interests around material and physical things. When clothes, and money, and social approval are accepted as our supreme values we must inevitably find death to be the absolute end of all we hold dear.

But the experience is different for those who are motivated by a higher ideal and purpose. They find joy in living. Every day is a challenge to service.

They carry the burden of those who are in need. They are not shaken by the thought of death because the major interest of their life is unbroken. The results of kindly service remain after death has done its worst.

Those who live by such an ideal are never obsessed by the feeling that death will sweep away everything for which they have striven. They have neither the time nor the inclination to think morbidly about the end of life, but if they think about it, it is without the emptiness of hope which stirs fear in the minds of those whose outlook is purely materialistic.

To keep life rich and abundant, that is important even when one retires from an occupation which has absorbed his interest and strength during his working years. One should try to make every day an adventure.

One woman who was victimized by fears of sickness and death came to ask her minister for spiritual help. In the conversation about the factors which caused her anxieties, the minister asked about her family background.

The woman said that her father had been during his lifetime the happiest person she had ever known. He had lived to be eighty-four years old, and had never experienced a serious illness.

When the minister inquired if she could explain why her father was such a happy man, she made no reply for a few moments. The question seemed to require careful consideration. Then at last she replied:

"During his last ten years he was happy because he had his family, his friends, and his garden. He seemed to keep on living so he could see his flowers bloom, or his grandchildren graduate from school. He always had something ahead to which he could look forward."

Death has no power to strike fear into the mind of such a man. His life is too full of experiences which are a part of the eternal plan which unfolds year by year.

See Death for What It Is

In the second place, if you are to have a faith to face the terminus of your earthly life, you must see death for what it is.

One day a man came to see me about making arrangements for his father's funeral service. In the course of our conversation he said: "I have a peculiar request to make of you. Could you conduct the service in such a way that you will not mention the word death?"

Before I could answer him, he went on to explain: "You see, my mother has a great fear of death, and even the mention of it sends terror through her soul. To her, death is the great enemy which finally overcomes life, and she does not want to think about it."

I told him that I had never had a funeral service in which I deleted all reference to death, but for his mother's sake, I would attempt to do so.

"But," I continued, "your mother has an entirely different conception of death from that which I hold, or, for that matter, which is taught by our Christian faith. Undoubtedly she thinks of life and death as being two separate states of being. One moment we are in a state of being called life, and the next we are in a state of being called death.

"But," I explained, "there is no state of being which we call death in our Christian faith, there is only life—life here and hereafter. And that which we call death is only a door which separates one phase of life from another phase of life, just as birth is the experience through which we pass from the pre-natal state of life to the post-natal state. Death is the name we give the door through which we pass from life to more life."

A few years before his death, John R. Mott was interviewed by the editor of a magazine. At the age of eighty-three years he was still traveling about the world from country to country on errands of mercy and righteousness.

A short time after the interview he was in China, making a study of the needs of those unfortunate people. This was before the Communists took over the unhappy country. The year before he had been one of the leaders at the World Council of Churches Assembly in Amsterdam.

After asking Dr. Mott some questions concerning his faith, the editor then asked the great Christian statesman this final question:

"Dr. Mott, what do you think death will be like?"

Said Dr. Mott: "I have given a great deal of thought

to that matter, and I must confess that I must be content with the expression of a personal opinion. I fear that a great many persons think of death as though it were the end of the journey. I do not, instead I think of it as a place where I change cars.

"You see," Dr. Mott continued, "all my life has been a journey. My secretary tells me that I have traveled more than two million miles. I have been at it for more than sixty years of my eighty-three years of life. And still I go on. I have a long way to go if I meet the responsibilities that still rest upon me.

"But I will not always be on the same train, the same ship, or the same plane. I will change conveyances and stations many times, but I shall go on. I guess that is what death means to me," Dr. Mott said. "It will be a place where I change cars, but I will go on. That seems to be the destiny God has marked for every man. And I will rejoice, for He will always be with me as He has been these sixty years of traveling. But I shall go on."

A Door into a Larger Life

Death holds no terrors for one who sees it for what it is—a swinging door opening into a larger life, a place to change cars for another destination—and always God is there to see us through the door, or on the car.

But of all who have walked the earth, it was Jesus of Nazareth who gave us the brightest gleam of light to guide us toward the Great Adventure. Just a few hours before His tragic death He said, "In my Father's house are many mansions, if it were not so, I would have told you, I go to prepare a place for you . . . Let not your heart be troubled, neither let it be afraid."

To multitudes in all ages since these words of faith in the continuity of life beyond the grave have brought consolation and courage. Standing by an open grave and having heard these words, who has not gone back to accept life with a stronger heart? They are not words of sorrow, but assurances of comfort and hope. There is the note of the "Hallelujah Chorus" in them!

Death is a going home to the Father's house, says Jesus. Why should we be afraid of going home? When He spoke those words of comfort and hope the Man of Galilee was Himself facing the prospect of that homegoing. And in that hour when men are honest with themselves, and seem to look with clearer insight into the mystery of things, He said that the next phase beyond this earthly existence is to be thought of in terms of home.

And when you live with that faith daily, you are able to face whatever may come to you in life with a steady heart. You are able to exhibit in your life the deep and wise words of Victor Hugo, when he wrote: "Courage for the great sorrows of life, and patience for the small ones, and then, when you have accomplished your daily task, go to sleep in peace, knowing that God is still awake."

Courage, my friend! Through life and in death, never lose heart!

G42